THE
BATHROOM
BLOOPERS
BOOK

by

Russ Edwards and Jack Kreismer

RED-LETTER PRESS, INC.
Saddle River, New Jersey

For information address:

Red-Letter Press, Inc.
P.O. Box 393, Saddle River, NJ 07458
www.Red-LetterPress.com

ACKNOWLEDGMENTS

Project Development Coordinator:
Kobus Reyneke

Cover design and typography:
s.w.artz, inc.

Editorial:
Jeff Kreismer

Disclaimer: We're flushed with pride to say that the items presented here are authentic. If you know otherwise, please advise us.

INTRODUCTION

"If we do not succeed, then we run the risk of failure."
-Dan Quayle

To err is human but *The Bathroom Bloopers Book* is a tribute
to those who have made truly superhuman efforts in the
pursuit of sappiness.

Included along with all the goofs and gaffes, mistakes and
misjudgments, the ill considered and the ill conceived, are
stories of just plain bad luck due to dumb circumstances
beyond anyone's control.

Read this book cover to cover or start at the middle and
work your way out. Pick any random page and you'll
probably find something amusing- it doesn't matter, we serve
up this sampler of stupidity in bite-sized chunks. And just as
the bathroom mirror doesn't always show you at your best,
you might see a little reflection of yourself in some of these
stories, so have compassion as you take your seat and save a
bit of the laughter for yourself. Always remember, it's a
blunder-ful life.

FOR AMERICA'S
FAVORITE READING ROOM

THE
BATHROOM
BLOOPERS
BOOK

*Weird and Wacky News
From the Bathroom
Hall of Shame*

THE BATHROOM LIBRARY

RED-LETTER PRESS, INC.
Saddle River, New Jersey

BATHROOM BLOOPER-TUBBY TAFT

325 pound William Taft was the biggest U.S. president. He was so big he once got stuck in the White House bathtub. It took four men to pry him out.

BLOOPER BRIEFS

A manager of a Seoul, South Korea, movie theater thought that the *Sound of Music* ran too long. He "corrected" the problem by cutting out the songs.

It was during the winter of 1979 when the Allied Roofing Company of Grand Rapids, Michigan, developed the business of cleaning off store rooftops of snow to prevent the heavy snowfall from collapsing the roofs. However, the company neglected to clean off its own roof and, yes, it collapsed.

The University of Arizona poison control center once treated a man who was bitten on the tongue while kissing a rattlesnake.

In 1971, an Arizona sportsman was out hunting when he accidentally shot himself in the leg. He went to call for help by firing off his rifle – and promptly shot himself in the other leg.

The following newspaper item comes from an edition of the *Philadelphia Inquirer*: "Donald Bollman was riding in a recreational vehicle with its owner when he asked to use the bathroom. His companion directed him to the rear, whereupon Bollman opened the moving vehicle's door and dropped out onto the Pennsylvania Turnpike."

When legendary TV news reporter Edward R. Murrow was a youngster, he bet a buddy that he could duck faster than the friend could fire a BB gun. Murrow lost the bet as the pellet hit him right between the eyes.

Franklin D. Roosevelt was a notorious practical joker, causing others to commit bloopers. At White House functions, the president realized that no one really paid attention to the brief pleasantries exchanged so on one occasion, as he shook hands with each guest he muttered, "I murdered my grandmother this morning." Only one guest, a Wall Street banker, responded. He said, "She certainly had it coming!"

A Mexican vegetarian health spa owner wrote in his will that he be buried only in the no-smoking section of the cemetery.

Publishing magnate Joseph Pulitzer once attempted to erect a billboard for his newspaper, *New York World*, that could be read from Mars. Alas, he gave up the project when he just couldn't figure out what language the Martians could read.

TINSELTOWN TIDBITS

Movie magnate Irving Thalberg explained that he didn't want to make *Gone with the Wind* because, "No Civil War picture ever made a nickel."

If at first you don't succeed ... The movie *Forrest Gump* was rejected for nine years and *One Flew Over the Cuckoo's Nest* for fifteen years! Both won Oscars for Best Picture.

The Muppet Show was banned in Turkey because TV executives there felt Miss Piggy would offend Muslims, who don't eat pork.

TV's *Weakest Link* host Anne Robinson: "Who wrote *Cat on a Hot Tin Roof*?"
Contestant: "Dr. Seuss."

"We don't like their sound, and guitar music is out."
Decca Recording Company, rejecting the Beatles in 1962.

Harry Cohn, the head of Columbia Pictures, dumped an aspiring actress in 1949 because he felt she had no star quality. Her name: Marilyn Monroe.

Reporter: "Now tell me, Britney, how do you feel about the meeting between George Bush and Tony Blair this week?"
Britney Spears: "Who's Tony Blair?"
Reporter: "He's the prime minister of Britain."
Spears: "Well, he must be a very important person."

"If I could drop dead now, I'd be the happiest man alive."
-Movie producer Samuel Goldwyn

Alfred Hitchcock's granddaughter once asked for the film director's help in writing a school paper to analyze one of his movies, *Shadow of a Doubt*. The teacher graded the paper a C.

Before Ed Sullivan became well known as the host of his own TV entertainment show on Sunday nights, he was a theater critic. In his very first review, he opined that playwright August Strindberg should consider rewriting the second act of his play *The Father*.

The only problem- Strindberg had been dead for almost a decade.

MISCELLANEOUS MISCREANT MAYHEM

A middle-aged woman in Lausanne, Switzerland, fainted in a supermarket and the call went out for medical help. A nurse arrived on the scene and decided to unhook the woman's bra so she could breathe better. After being unfastened, a shoplifted frozen chicken was discovered in the bra. The nurse concluded the woman had fainted from the cold.

Michael Robinson, an employee of a restaurant in Americus, Georgia, got a credit card number of a customer and went on a short shopping spree in 1997. He was caught soon after purchasing $45.27 worth of compact discs from a music store. Much to his surprise, he was arrested by Secret Service agents. You see, the credit card number he'd stolen belonged to Jimmy Carter.

A Santa Cruz, California, pharmacist opened his place one morning only to find a pair of legs dangling from the ceiling inside the shop. He found a crook who was trapped in a ceiling vent.

When the police arrived, the thug explained that he was walking his dog on the roof of the drug store and had accidentally fallen through. He was arrested, anyway.

According to *Point of View*, published by the Alameda
County (California) District Attorney's office, a crook walked
into an Oakland bank and handed a teller a note which read,
"This is a stickup. Hand over all yer mony fast."

Noticing that the guy appeared to be no nuclear physicist,
the teller said, "I'll hand over the cash as long as you sign for
it. It's a bank policy: All robbers have to sign for their money."

The crook thought it over and said, "Uh, I guess that's okay."

He signed his full name and address and that's where the
police found him a bit later on.

A West Haven, Connecticut, man was arrested after a cop
stopped him near a WaWa convenience store that had just
been robbed. When the arresting policeman asked the man
what he'd been doing, the guy replied, "I just left the WaWa
store that I robbed."

When questioned about a theft at Lakeside Deli and Mini
Market in Middlefield, Connecticut, suspect Frank Margary
told detectives, "There's no way (the clerk) could identify me.
I had my hat down over my eyes."

The FBI reports that, on average, 45 bank robbers are
arrested each year because they were dumb enough to write
their holdup notes on the back of their own deposit slips.

A bank teller in Swansea, Massachusetts, told the stick-up man she had no money. He fainted and was still unconscious when the cops arrived. Then, when they found his getaway car, the cops discovered the keys were locked inside it.

A would-be Chicago robber grabbed a manhole cover from the street, smashed a jewelry store window, snatched the gems from inside and would have made a clean getaway except for one thing- he fell down the open manhole.

In Union City, California, a burglar was surprised by the homeowner's return so he ran out of the house, jumped over a fence and wound up in the neighbor's yard. The crook, who knows why, was butt naked and quickly apprehended because his jump over the fence landed him in a cactus garden.

In Lake City, Florida, a woman was arrested for trying to hold up a Howard Johnson Motel with a chain saw. Unfortunately for the would-be thief, the chain saw was electric and it wasn't plugged in.

In Boulder, Colorado, in 1989, postal inspectors found that one of their mail carriers had buried 6,500 pounds of mail in his backyard instead of delivering it.

In Newark, New Jersey, a thief who was babysitting his four-year old daughter, broke into a home and stole several things, but there was one thing he left behind – his kid.

A crook was arrested after he was caught burglarizing a home in Martinsville, Indiana. The thug was discovered when he started playing the owner's piano and didn't stop until the cops got there.

Cops in Redondo Beach, California, noticed a white Mazda being driven erratically down the Pacific Coast Highway. Even more suspicious, the upper half of a traffic-light pole was lying across the car's hood. When they pulled the car over, the obviously inebriated driver's explanation for the pole was, "It came with the car when I bought it."

SPORTS SHORTS

Former Utah Jazz power forward Karl Malone said this in defense of fellow hoopster Charles Barkley: "Say what you want about Charles Barkley, when he tells you he is going to do something he'll either do it or he won't."

"You have to have a catcher because, if you don't, the pitch will roll all the way back to the screen."
-Manager Casey Stengel

"Winfield goes back to the wall and it rolls off! It's rolling all the way to back to second base! This is a terrible thing for the Padres!"

-San Diego announcer Jerry Coleman

"Can you lower my taxes, please? I was really unhappy with my tax bracket. I work hard and I want to keep my earnings."

-Venus Williams, U.S. Open tennis champ, in a phone conversation with President Bill Clinton

"(Babe) Ruth made a great mistake when he gave up pitching. Working once a week, he might have lasted a long time and become a great star."

-Cleveland Indians manager-outfielder Tris Speaker, in 1912

Ozzie Guillen, former Chicago White Sox shortstop, said, "When I struggle at the plate, I ask the trainer for eye drops and I put them right on my bat so my bat can see the ball good."

"If I wake up one morning and decide another person can do a better job with this squad, I will tell the wife, 'Let's go to Italy-or Brooklyn.' Either one of those countries is fine with me."

-Penn State football coach Joe Paterno

"Mickey Mantle's a switch-hitter because he's amphibious."
   -Yogi Berra

"You wouldn't have won if we had beaten you."
   -Yogi Berra

"George Hendrick simply lost that sun-blown pop-up."
   -San Diego Padres announcer Jerry Coleman

"Grubb goes back ... back ... He's under the warning track."
   -San Diego Padres announcer Jerry Coleman

"Larry Lintz steals second standing up. He slid, but he didn't have to."
   -Jerry Coleman, San Diego Padres announcer

"Hi folks, I'm Jerry Gross. No, I'm not, I'm Jerry Coleman."
   -San Diego Padres announcer Jerry Coleman

"Sometimes they write what I say and not what I mean."
   *-Pedro Guerrero, St. Louis Cardinals,
   on sportswriters*

"Pitching is 80% of the game. The other half is hitting and fielding."

-Mickey Rivers, Texas Rangers outfielder

"Last night I neglected to mention something that bears repeating."

-Ron Fairly, San Francisco Giants announcer

"It was pretty good. Even the music was nice."

-Yogi Berra, after attending an opera

"Nobody in football should be called a genius. A genius is a guy like Norman Einstein."

-Joe Theismann, ex-quarterback and TV analyst

"Bob Lemon is going to be our manager all year. You can bet on it. I don't care if we come in last. I swear on my heart he'll be the manager all season."

-Yankees owner George Steinbrenner ...
Fourteen games later, Lemon was fired.

"I have nothing to say. And I'll only say it once."

-Floyd Smith, Toronto Maple Leafs coach

"Twelve for 23 ... It doesn't take a genius to see that's under 50 percent."

-Dick Vitale, basketball TV analyst

"Do they have my number? I don't know. Do they have a guy with the number 35?"

-Kansas City Chiefs running back Christian Okoye, when asked if the Denver Broncos had his number

Kent Hrbek, former first sacker for the Minnesota Twins, embarrassingly admits to this one. "Mike Easler (of the Yankees) was leading off first. I bent over, waiting for a possible pickoff throw from the pitcher, when I farted right in Easler's face. On the next pitch, Easler took his lead- while holding his nose."

Golfer Wayne Grady was disqualified from the Phoenix Open on January 26, 1986, for playing someone else's ball. At the Los Angeles Open a month later, he did it again.

"Right now I have three C's: comfortable, confident, and seeing the ball well."

-Jay Buhner, Seattle Mariners outfielder

In the puckering up department, Randy Pierce, a right wing with the Colorado Rockies hockey team at the time, scored an insurance goal against the New York Islanders in a 7-4 win on November 28, 1979. Pierce was so pleased with himself that he retrieved the puck, kissed it and then tossed it into the crowd. He was assessed a two-minute penalty for delay of game.

In the 1976 Olympics fencing event, a Soviet army major was disqualified for rigging his sword with a circuit breaker to register a hit on an opponent without actually making one.

Former Oakland A's pitcher Dave Stewart created a game he called, "Master Pain." The winner is the hurler in the bullpen who can stand the most pain. Said Stewart, "You sit there and pull hairs out of each other's nose. Is that wacky enough for you?"

Hillary Clinton (at the time, running for a New York senate seat): "The fact is, I've always been a Yankee fan."

Katie Couric (co-host of the *Today Show*): "I thought you were a Cubs fan."

Clinton: "I am. I am a Cubs fan."

"I'm really happy for Coach Cooper and the guys who've been around here for six or seven years, especially our seniors."
-Bob Hoying, Ohio State quarterback,
after winning a Big Ten title

"We lost because we didn't win."
-Soccer superstar Ronaldo

Los Angeles Kings hockey player Craig Rodenfels hurled a live chicken in a Kings uniform onto the ice during a 1988 regular season game. This fowl move resulted in his ejection from the game and Rodenfels was also arrested on a charge of malicious mischief and cruelty to animals.

In 1989, Ohio's Central State University awarded Mike Tyson an honorary doctorate in humane letters at its commencement ceremonies. Accepting the award, Tyson said, "I don't know what kind of doctor I am, but watching all of these beautiful sisters here, I'm debating whether I should be a gynecologist."

At the 1959 Memphis Invitational Open, golfer Tommy Bolt was fined $250 for "letting one loose" as an opponent was just about to tee off.

In 1990, Atlanta Braves pitcher John Smoltz incurred second-degree burns on his chest when he tried to iron a shirt while he was wearing it.

"A gun is like a recreational tool – like a golf club or tennis racket. You can kill someone with a golf club, you know."
        -NRA official Martel Lovelace

On May 25, 1993, Texas outfielder Jose Canseco drifted back on a deep fly ball hit by Cleveland's Carlos Martinez. The ball bounced off Canseco's noggin and went over the fence for a homer. Oh, and a few days later, Canseco tried his hand at pitching. He blew out his right elbow and needed surgery.

On October 26, 1964, Minnesota Vikings defensive end Jim Marshall recovered a fumble by the San Francisco 49ers at their own 34-yard line. Unfortunately, Marshall began running the wrong way- all the way to the end zone for a safety.

In July 2003, Portland Trail blazer guard Damon Stoudamire was arrested with more than 40 grams of marijuana in his possession. The pot was found when he set off an airport metal detector after walking through the security area- with his weed wrapped in foil.

First baseman Marvelous Marv Throneberry was one of the original "Amazin" Mets- amazingly inept, that it. At skipper Casey Stengel's birthday party, Marv asked why he wasn't given a piece of cake. Casey answered, "We'd have given you a piece but we were afraid you'd drop it." On another occasion, Throneberry hit a triple but was called out for missing first base. When Stengel went out to argue the call, one of his coaches stopped him and said, "Don't bother, Casey. He missed second, too."

In a 1934 ball game at Philadelphia's Baker Field, Brooklyn manager Casey Stengel went to the mound to remove his pitcher, Boom Boom Beck. So irate at being taken out of the game, Beck fired the ball at the rightfield wall. Outfielder Hack Wilson, as the story goes, was badly hung over from a night on the town and not really into the action. He heard the sound of the ball hitting the fence, raced to the ball and hurled a perfect strike to second to nail the phantom baserunner.

COOKED COOK

According to a 1988 edition of the *San Francisco Chronicle*, a chef accidentally cooked his salary.

He was working in the kitchen of the New House Hotel, in Haverdfordwest, Wales, one night. When it came time to close the place, he was too tired to climb up the stairs to where the hotel safe was located so he put his wages in the oven. When he arrived at work the next morning, he forgot that the oven wasn't empty, turned it on and the rest is history.

HIGH WIRE ACT

It was during a parade in Ventura, California, when a drum major threw his baton as high as he could. The baton struck an overhead power line which caused a 10-block power outage, put a radio station off the air and started a grass fire.

BATHROOM BLOOPER

As reported by the *Jerusalem Post*, a Tel Aviv, Israel, woman squashed a cockroach and tossed it in the toilet. She then polished off an entire can of bug spray into the toilet to complete the job.

Sometime later, her husband went to the bathroom and sat down on the toilet while smoking a cigarette. When he finished smoking, he tossed the lit cigarette into the toilet. You can guess what happened next. The lit cigarette caused the insecticide fumes to explode, resulting in severe burns on the man's "private parts."

To make matters worse, ambulance workers called upon the scene placed the man on a stretcher. When the injured man told them what had happened, they convulsed in laughter and dropped the stretcher, cracking his pelvis and breaking two of the poor fellow's ribs.

CHAINSAW MASSACRE

In July of 1976, Eugene Schneider of Carteret, New Jersey, was divorced. The court ordered that he and his wife divide their property equally. Schneider took the order quite literally as he took a chainsaw and cut the couple's $80,000 home in two.

SIGNS OF THE TIMES

"Please do not feed the animals. Give all food to the guard on duty."

-Sign at the Budapest zoo

"Toilet out of order. Please use floor below."

-Sign in a London office

"Please do not touch this exhibit."

-A brass plate with Braille writing for the blind at a London museum

"When this sign is under water, this road is impassable."

-On a Burmese river road

"Sign up and have a happy new rear."

-Holiday sign outside a Chicago health club

"We exchange anything – bicycles, washing machines, etc. Why not bring your wife along and get a wonderful bargain?"

-Sign outside a secondhand shop

"No children allowed."

-In an Indian maternity ward

"Antique Tables Made Here Daily."

-Outside a northern Virginia furniture store

MR. POTATO HEAD

During a 1987 Eastern League game between the Williamsport Bills and the Reading Phillies, catcher Dave Bresnahan tried to throw out a runner with a potato. In a phony pickoff attempt, the bush league catcher hurled what looked like a genuine baseball over the outstretched glove of the third baseman. It was actually a potato Bresnahan had carved up to look like a baseball. When the base runner darted for home, Bresnahan was holding the real ball and tagged him out, or so he thought. The runner was called safe and Bresnahan was ejected. The next day he was fined $50 by Williamsport and subsequently released by the Bills' parent club, the Cleveland Indians, on grounds of "unprofessional" conduct.

"HIGH-JINX"

Frank Perkins of San Jose, California, maintained that he could sit atop a 60-foot flagpole for a year. He actually stayed up for some 400 days. However, he had a real comedown afterwards when he learned that, during his stint in the air, the company which hired him for the stunt went bankrupt. Not only that, Perkins' electricity and phone were turned off for non-payment of bills. To top it off, his girlfriend left him for another guy.

DEAD WRONG

In 1978, defendant Raymond Thompson took the stand in Philadelphia's Common Pleas court to answer charges of robbery and assault. He explained to the court that he couldn't possibly be guilty because he was dead.

COMEDY IN THE COURT

*The following "Q and A's" were taken
from courtroom proceedings.*

Q: Did you blow your horn or anything?
A: After the accident?
Q: Before the accident.
A: Sure, I played for ten years. I even went to school for it.

Q: What was the first thing your husband said to you
when he woke that morning?
A: He said, "Where am I, Cathy?"
Q: And why did that upset you?
A: My name is Susan.

Q: How many trucks do you own?
A: Seventeen.
Q: Seventy?
A: Seventeen.
Q. Seventeen?
A: No, about twelve.

Q: This myasthenia gravis – does it affect your memory at all?
A: Yes.
Q: And in what ways does it affect your memory.
A: I forget.

Q: Doctor, how many autopsies have you performed on
dead people?
A: All my autopsies are performed on dead people.

Q: She had three children, right?
A: Yes.
Q: How many were boys?
A: None.
Q: Were there any girls?

Q: Doctor, did you say he was shot in the woods?
A: No, I said he was shot in the lumbar region.

Q: What is your name?
A: Ernestine McDowell.
Q: And what is your marital status?
A: Fair.

Q: Could you see him from where you were standing?
A: I could see his head.
Q: And where was his head?
A: Just above his shoulders.

Q: Do you know how far pregnant you are right now?
A: I will be three months November 8th.
Q: Apparently then, the date of conception was August 8th?
A: Yes.
Q: What were you and your husband doing at that time?

Q: What happened then?
A: He told me, he says, "I have to kill you because you can identify me."
Q: Did he kill you?
A: No.

Q: Were you acquainted with the deceased?
A: Yes, sir.
Q: Before or after he died?

Q: And, officer, was your radar unit functioning correctly
    at the time you had the plaintiff on radar?
A: Yes, it was malfunctioning correctly.

Q: Trooper, when you stopped the defendant, were your
    red and blue lights flashing?
A: Yes.
Q: Did the defendant say anything when she got out of
    the car?
A: Yes, sir.
Q: What did she say?
A: What disco am I at?

Q: And lastly, Gary, all your responses must be oral, OK?
A: OK.
Q: What school did you go to?
A: Oral.

IF THE SHOE FITS...

It was in August 1978 when Seattle police searched a
suspicious 27-year-old man's apartment. They found a bag
which contained 65 unmatched women's shoes. The guy lived
within a half a block of where many women had complained of
being knocked down by a man who then grabbed one of their
shoes and took off.

WARNING TAGS

The funniest thing about warning tags is speculating about the circumstances that required them in the first place. Behind every warning label there are two things: a blithering idiot and a lawyer with a new beach house.

Here's a new wrinkle on warning tags-a steam iron that carries this warning: "Never iron clothes while they are being worn."

No comment on the digital thermometer that carries the precaution: "Once used rectally, the thermometer should not be used orally."

Your parenting skills need to be worked on if you really need this warning tag on a baby stroller: "Remove child before folding." Ditto for this one on a snow sled: "Beware: sled may develop high speed under certain snow conditions." Or even this one on a kitchen appliance: "Do not allow children to play in the dishwasher."

It's hearth-warming to know they care. A well-known quick light fireplace log warns the user: "Caution - Risk of Fire."

More rigorous civil defense drills are called for when a Taiwan manufacturer needs to put a warning label on a blanket that states:
"Not to be used as protection from a tornado."

You've got to ask if the airline considers their passengers are a few goobers short of a nut cluster when they serve a bag of peanuts marked: "Instructions - open packet, eat nuts."

Bowl Fresh, though a fine product, seems overly concerned about the permissive parents among their clientele. They saw fit to attach the following warning: "Safe to use around pets and children, although it is not recommended that either be permitted to drink from toilet."

The manual of a chainsaw states offhandedly: "Do not attempt to stop the blade with your hand."

Someone apparently had a bone to pick with a pet products manufacturer when they put this warning on a bottle of shampoo for dogs: "Caution: The contents of this bottle should not be fed to fish."

You might be thinking "refund" when you read this statement on your can of self-defense pepper spray: "Caution- May irritate eyes."

One would hope consumers would get the picture from the following reminder on a camera: "This camera only works when there is film inside."

Somebody has taken the term "channel-surfing" way too literally when they have to print on a TV remote control: "Not dishwasher safe."

That "Save water- shower together" campaign went too far when a hotel-provided shower cap has to specify: "Fits one head."

And, oh yes, consider yourself warned: *The Bathroom Bloopers Book* is not to be used for personal hygiene- "Severe paper cuts may result from the misuse of this product."

INSURANCE INSANITY

Here are some actual excerpts from auto insurance claims.

"Coming home, I drove into the wrong house and collided with a tree I don't have."

"I saw the slow-moving, sad-faced old gentleman as he bounced off the hood of my car."

"I was taking my canary to the hospital. It got loose in the car and flew out the window. The next thing I saw was his rear end, and there was a crash."

"I was thrown from my car as it left the road. I was later found in a ditch by some stray cows."

"To avoid hitting the bumper of the car in front, I struck the pedestrian."

"An invisible car came out of nowhere, struck my vehicle, and vanished."

"In my attempt to kill a fly, I struck a telephone pole."

"The guy was all over the road. I had to swerve a number of times before I hit him."

"The pedestrian had no idea which direction to go, so I ran over him."

"I had been shopping for plants all day and was on my way home. As I reached an intersection, a hedge sprung up, obscuring my vision."

BATHROOM BLOOPER- IN A LATHER

The very thing Ivory Soap bars are most famous for resulted from a lucky mistake. The factory had been over-mixing the soap formula causing excess air bubbles that made it float. Customers wrote and told the soap makers how much they liked that the bars floated and the soap has floated ever since.

WAR STORIES

During the Civil War, Union General Ambrose Burnside had a brilliant idea for breaking through the Confederate defenses at Petersburg, Virginia. He ordered that a long tunnel be dug under the enemy lines and then packed with explosives. It took weeks but it was finally accomplished and the fuse lit.

No one on either side had ever seen such an explosion as the 500-foot "mine" blew sky high, scattering the rebel troops from their positions as predicted.

Congratulations were passed among the Union officers for about half-an-hour before the troops finally charged across the gap.

That was mistake number one. The delay had given the Confederates time to gather their wits and move back to their positions.

Mistake number two was when the Union men did charge, they were led down into the 30-foot deep pit rather than around it. As the Southern boys now held the high ground and the officers in charge of the Federal troops had neglected to bring ladders, it was a bad day for the Union. Burnside left the army (probably the greatest service to his country he could perform) and naturally, a little over a year later, he was kicked upstairs to Governor of Rhode Island.

Japan's Hiroo Onoda carried on World War II almost 29 years after the other combatants kissed and made up.

Onoda was finally captured on March 10, 1974, in the Philippines, still fighting for Japan despite a total absence of any enemy troops for several decades.

It took a further six months to convince the man that the war was actually over and he had spent the best years of his life hiding in a jungle for no good reason. Oh well, at least he set a record.

Actually, Onoda was cheated out of even that accolade when in December 1974, Teruo Nakamura was discovered holding out on the island of Morotai and Onoda, the man who had battled on for his Emperor for so long, was relegated to second place.

TEXAS TWO-"FER"

Big Spring, Texas, police received a report of a stolen car and a complete description. A model of law-enforcement efficiency, a short time later they spotted the car and pulled it over. As fate would have it, the guy who phoned in the report was nearby and hurried over to identify the car.

That's when the Big Spring police got even more efficient. Upon checking the tags, they discovered that the guy who phoned in the stolen car report had, in fact, stolen it himself.

GREAT MOMENTS IN CORPORATE STUPIDITY

POP FIZZLE

On April 23rd, 1985, the Coca Cola Company introduced New Coke. That in itself wasn't necessarily a major blooper but the company did manage to qualify for the Four Flush Folly Award by discontinuing original Coke, a worldwide favorite for the better part of a century.

When sales of New Coke went flat in the marketplace, executives were forced to bring back the original some months later, calling it "Coke Classic." Some conspiracy theorists, however, attribute the whole affair to Coke's plan to dodge high sugar prices and re-introduce the product with cheaper sweeteners. It's more fun to consider the whole incident stupid rather than sinister so when it comes to bloopers, here's to Coke, it's the real thing.

PARIAH CAREY

EMI forked over a $21 million signing bonus to Mariah Carey for an $80 million deal to record five albums. After the first album, EMI paid her another $28 million to not record any further albums. Stockholders take note: that means your company paid out $49 million for the soundtrack to *Glitter*.

ANATOMICALLY AND POLITICALLY INCORRECT

The people at Mattel have built many a Dream House with the profits from Barbie since 1960. But then it happened-Barbie, at 43, had a mid-life crisis. The toymaker announced that she was dumping Ken, with whom she had gone steady for decades. She now was getting jiggy with Blaine- an Aussie surfer of dubious prospects. The resulting scandal caused the sales to plummet precipitously. Don't worry about Ken, though, he'll land on his feet. Maybe he'll romance someone with even more plastic than Barbie- Cher.

DO NOT PASS GO

When Charles Darrow first brought his get-rich game of Monopoly to Parker Brothers during the Depression, they rejected the game out of hand as being "too complicated." They therefore almost missed their chance at what was to become the best-selling board game of all time.

BEAN COUNTERS

Hormel Foods had to recall 104,000 pounds of Stagg canned chili. According to the label, the cans contained "hearty beef with a kick of green chilies." What it didn't mention was that the batch in question also held parts of a handheld computer in tasty byte-sized chunks.

KEELHAULED

On Lake Isabella in the high desert east of Bakersfield, California, a woman brought her boat into a marina complaining that it was sluggish. The normally nimble Bayliner was wallowing like a garbage scow.

A quick check of the deck and engine showed everything was shipshape and the marina guys were temporarily stumped. It was when they went down into the water and examined the hull that the mystery was solved- the boat was still firmly attached to its trailer.

STROKES OF GENIUS-
A GRAB BAG OF GOLF GOOFS
AND GAFFES

THE WRONG CUP...

Sam Snead once drove a ball into the pocket of a man who was standing nearly 250 yards away but Homero Blancas topped him when his ball bounced off a palm tree and landed in the bra of a spectator. Blancas conferred with Chi Chi Rodriguez as to what he should do and Rodriguez advised, "I think you should play it."

SUPER BLOOPER

While playing the qualifying round of the Shawnee Invitational For Ladies in 1912, one hapless lass knocked her tee shot into the Binniekill River. The ball floated a mile and a half downstream before she managed to get another whack at it. She finally finished the 130-yard 16th by taking 166 strokes for the hole!

PALMER'S PUTTS

Covering a big golf match, a breathless announcer whispered, "Arnie Palmer is getting ready to putt. Arnie, usually a great putter, seems to be having trouble with his long putt. However he is having no trouble with his shorts." At another match, the announcer informed the world, "Johnny Tee is now on the pot -err, I mean Johnny Pott is now on the tee..."

SLICE- PRESIDENT

Though Gerald Ford is famed for his golfing mishaps, former vice-president Spiro Agnew also racked up an impressive body count. On February 13th, 1971, Agnew hit both a husband and wife with just one shot. On his next swing he took out a woman spectator by bopping her on the ankle. Since he was thoroughly warmed up, he went out the next day and cracked Doug Sanders in the noggin. Bob Hope said of Agnew, "He can't cheat on his scorecard- all you have to do to find out the number of strokes he took is look down the fairway and count the bodies!"

FORE!-HEAD

Mac McLendon wasn't doing very well in the first round of the 1979 Masters. He was possessed by an eerie feeling, a premonition that he was going to hit someone with his ball. That night he shared his fear with his wife, Joan. A good and dutiful golf wife, she reassured him and gave him the confidence to go out the next day. Freed of his apprehensions, he knew he'd play better. He confidently strode up to the first hole and with his very first swing, he managed to conk a spectator - his wife Joan!

A REAL PUTTS

A.J. Lewis holds the record for the most putts on a single green. Back in 1890, he required 156 putts to drop the ball in the cup.

WEAR TWO PAIR OF GOLF PANTS-
YOU MAY GET A HOLE IN ONE

Golfer Bob Russell took a practice shot on a municipal course in Ohio in 1974 and felt a terrible pain in his leg. The head of his driver hit a bullet that someone had carelessly left behind. Fortunately the wound was minor although it did ruin a perfectly good pair of golf pants.

HEAD INJURY

Some days it doesn't pay to get out of bed. Such was the case for Owen E. Cummings who found himself in four inches of water behind a stone wall. Owen took a mighty swing and topped the ball which bounced off the wall and into the cup for an eagle 3. Unfortunately, the club head also hit the wall, flew off and ricocheted back into his face, knocking him cold. Although he won the hole, he was carried off the course and forfeited the game.

IN THE DRINK

Bill Blair and Harry Webb had parked their golf cart on a hill at Indiana's Valley View Golf Club and walked over to the 11th tee. Before they could tee off, there was a loud bang. As they looked around they saw their golf cart roll down the hill and become submersed when it crashed into the pond below. Seems a nearby golfer drove his ball into the cart's accelerator, releasing the brake. With the help of scuba divers and a tractor, the pair was able to get the cart and most of their clubs back.

BUMBLING BUREAUCRATS

CATCHING THE BUS- LITERALLY

While the US was celebrating 200 years of independence in 1976, our erstwhile rulers over in Jolly Olde England were still demonstrating the same sort of forethought and judgment that outfitted their soldiers in bright red coats whilst fighting a war in mostly wooded terrain. In this case, the easy target was a Staffordshire Councilor who explained to angry riders that the reason that the Hanley-Bagnall busses no longer stopped to pick up any passengers whatsoever was that to do so would seriously impact the efficiency of the bus schedule.

PI'S UP

In 1897, the General Assembly of Indiana passed a law which officially set the value of pi at 4. As this constant represents the ratio of a circle's circumference to its diameter, it is critical to all engineering projects and is usually taken to be 3.1416. In fact, pi is often calculated to even more decimal places to ensure accuracy. This pretty much guaranteed that any projects using the official value would be horribly botched. Be especially careful of driving over any old Indiana bridges built during that era.

FROM THE "MAKE LOVE, NOT WAR" DEPARTMENT:

It's reported that Uncle Sam once considered building a bomb that would render enemy soldiers sexually irresistible to one another. Would they have named it the "Don't Ask, Don't Tell Shell"?

FROM ILLEGAL SPEAKEASIES
TO ILLEGAL TO SPEAK ENGLISH...

Back in 1935, Chicago Mayor Bill Thompson had a law passed that forbade speaking "English." Loyal citizens were to speak only "American."

JERSEY JUSTICE

In New Jersey it is illegal to delay or detain a homing pigeon. In Ocean City, slurping soup can land you in the hoosegow and in the Jersey state capital, Trenton, never but never throw a bad pickle in the street or you'll be in one.

RAZING THE ROOF

A Thai restaurant in Perth, Australia, had a cockroach problem and something had to be done.

Employees laid out a dozen bug bombs. Eight would have been enough for a complete fumigation but figuring that it's better to be safe than sorry, they added a dozen more. And since the wily cockroach had survived all challenges for the past 400 million years, who could argue with a bit of overkill? And so yet another dozen bug bombs were pressed into service.

When the 36 fumigators were unleashed at once, the restaurant did briefly become a bug-free zone. Unfortunately, moments later, the concentrated fumes reached a pilot light in the kitchen and the resulting explosion rendered it a restaurant-free zone as well.

MORE MISCREANT MISBEHAVIOR

WIRETRAPPED

Two Rogersville, Tennessee, ne're-do-wells gave new meaning to the term "cell phone" after their phone landed them in a cell.

It seems that as they were plotting a crime, one of the would-be crooks bumped the speed dial button on the phone in his pocket. As luck would have it, it was the 911 button. The police heard the whole conversation and nabbed the suspects. Oh, by the way, it happened on April Fools' Day.

A GAS ATTACK

The price of gas is enough to make you sick. At least it was for one Seattle crook who attempted to siphon gas from a large motor home. Police report that the plan went down the drain about the same time as the suspect's siphon hose went likewise into the camper's sewage tank instead of the fuel tank.

Naturally, to get the siphon started, the would-be Public Enemy Number One and Two used his mouth to apply suction at the end of the hose. Seconds later he sentenced himself to cruel and unusual punishment as he caught a healthy mouthful of human high-test. The shock caused him to swallow and he fell on the ground choking as the fluid continued to flow all over and around him. He was so pitiful by the time the police arrived that the motor home's owner refused to press charges claiming that it was the best laugh he'd ever had.

THIS CRIME DOESN'T PAY ANYWAY

Down south in Cajun-country, a man wlked into a Circle-K, slapped a $20 bill on the counter and asked for change. When the clerk opened the cash drawer, the man pulled a gun and demanded all the money in the register. The thief took it and absconded with his loot but forgot the $20 bill on the counter. Since the money in the cash drawer only amounted to $15 the crook was down five bucks on the deal. Might that be referred to as an "ill-gotten loss"?

LOW-SPEED PURSUIT

Perhaps it's not as exciting as a white Ford Bronco but a man led Los Angles police on quite a chase driving a stolen steamroller. Reaching speeds of 5 mph flat out (pardon the pun), the chase came to an end when the suspect just coasted to a stop. He apparently took the vehicle simply because he was tired of walking.

CROOK GETS CRASH COURSE

An Ohio thief had high-flying aspirations when he stole several pieces of expensive equipment from an airplane in Knox County.

Among the gadgets he removed, however, was the plane's Emergency Locating Transmitter used to find a plane in the event of a crash.

The crook banged it around enough to trigger the automatic beacon and was soon grounded by police who traced the signal right to his lair.

CHURCH BULLETIN BOARD BLOOPERS

*Enjoy this unholy collection of
ministry misprints and ecclesiastical errata…*

"The cost for attending the Fasting and Prayer conference includes meals."

"Ladies, don't forget the rummage sale. It's a chance to get rid of those things not worth keeping around the house. Don't forget your husbands."

"Potluck supper Sunday at 5:00 pm - prayer and medication to follow."

"Eight new choir robes are currently needed, due to the addition of several new members and to the deterioration of some older ones."

"Don't let worry kill you - let the Church help."

"Ladies Bible Study will be held Thursday morning at 10 am. All ladies are invited to lunch in the Fellowship Hall after the B.S. is done."

"Pastor is on vacation. Massages can be given to church secretary."

"This evening at 7 pm there will be a hymn sing in the park across from the Church. Bring a blanket and come prepared to sin."

"A bean supper will be held on Tuesday evening in the church hall. Music will follow."

"The Low Self-Esteem Support Group will meet Thursday at 7 pm. Please use the back door."

"The Associate Minister unveiled the church's new tithing campaign slogan last Sunday: 'I Upped My Pledge - Now Up Yours.'"

"A new loudspeaker system has been installed in the church. It was given by one of our members in honor of his wife."

"Weight Watchers will meet at 7 pm at the First Presbyterian Church. Please use the large double door at the side entrance."

"The ladies of the Church have cast off clothing of every kind. They may be seen in the basement on Friday afternoon."

DAN QUAYLE- NEED WE SAY MORE?

According to the *New Republic*, when Dan Quayle was to fill a vacancy on the National Space Council, he got author Tom Clancy on board as an unpaid consultant. As illustrious as he is though, Clancy was Quayle's second choice. His first choice for the position was a famed space pioneer from the 60's. The Vice President's plan to approach the aviator with the honor was scuttled, however, when Dan discovered that Clutch Cargo was, in fact, entirely fictional and a cartoon character to boot.

EXTRA! EXTRA! READ ALL ABOUT IT!

Real Hilarious Headlines…

IRAQI HEAD SEEKS ARMS

LIGHT MEALS ARE LOWER IN FAT, CALORIES

PROSTITUTES APPEAL TO POPE

CONCEALED WEAPONS CHARGES FILED
AGAINST NUDE DANCER

STUDY FINDS SEX, PREGNANCY LINK

NJ JUDGE TO RULE ON NUDE BEACH

STIFF OPPOSITION EXPECTED
TO CASKETLESS FUNERAL PLAN

TEEN-AGE GIRLS OFTEN HAVE BABIES
FATHERED BY MEN

BIBLE CHURCH'S FOCUS IS THE BIBLE

IS THERE A RING OF DEBRIS AROUND URANUS?

TOMATOES COME IN BIG, LITTLE, MEDIUM SIZES

INFERTILITY UNLIKELY TO BE PASSED ON

LACK OF BRAINS HINDERS RESEARCH

HOSPITALS ARE SUED BY 7 FOOT DOCTORS

PANDA MATING FAILS; VETERINARIAN TAKES OVER

MAN STRUCK BY LIGHTNING
FACES BATTERY CHARGE

RENEWED FIGHTING THREATENS PEACE

BOYS CAUSE AS MANY PREGNANCIES AS GIRLS

NEW STUDY OF OBESITY
LOOKS FOR LARGER TEST GROUP

ANTIQUE STRIPPER
TO DEMONSTRATE WARES AT STORE

ASTRONAUT TAKES BLAME FOR GAS IN SPACECRAFT

FISH LURK IN STREAMS

THE PUNISHMENT FITS THE CRIME

A man in Bristol, England, craved a lobster dinner but didn't want to shell out for the pricey crustaceans so he hatched a shoplifting plot that would get him in more hot water than the lobsters.

Pretty much all you have to know is that the crime involved hiding two lobsters in his pants. In retrospect, he no doubt regretted not making sure that the rubber bands restricting their claws were securely in place.

In this case it wasn't the long arm of the law which proved to be his undoing. Paramedics eventually pried off the lobsters but not before they assured that the miscreant would not be able to pass his criminal proclivities on to future generations.

MISDIRECTION

A budding criminal genius was brought down in Plainview, Connecticut, just because he didn't realize the Devil in the details.

His plan was to hold up a Dairy Mart. To ensure that he had clear sailing, on his way there, he called 911 and reported a robbery at another Dairy Mart on the far side of town.

Pretty clever? Yes, indeed, but as if to prove that there's no such thing as the perfect crime, he screwed up and gave the police not the address of the Dairy Mart across town but the very one he had targeted. The cops were prompt, he was nabbed in the act and no doubt was given a few years to review his error.

QUAYLEISMS

A selection of quizzical quotes from the former VP,
Dan Quayle, who proved once and for all,
it's a blunderful life…

"They asked me to go in front of the Reagans. I'm not used to going in front of President Reagan, so we went out behind the Bushes."
> *- after the swearing-in ceremony on*
> *Inauguration Day*

"The President scores much better than Bill Clinton."
> *- comparing George Bush's record to Clinton's*
> *during an interview with David Frost*

"For NASA, space is still a high priority."
> *- during a speech to NASA employees*

"What a waste it is to lose one's mind. Or not to have a mind is being very wasteful. How true that is."
> *- speaking to the United Negro College Fund*

"I love California. I practically grew up in Phoenix."

"I was recently on a tour of Latin America, and the only regret I have was that I didn't study Latin harder in school so I could converse with those people."

"I stand by all the misstatements that I've made."

BATHROOM BLOOPERS
FOUR FLUSH SALUTES

"Good judgment comes from experience, and experience comes from bad judgment."
- *Barry LePatner*

*Here we honor those blunders
that have gone down the drain in a big way...*

(SOFTWARE CATEGORY)

One of the great threats to the bottom line in the recording industry is the unauthorized copying and the subsequent sharing of the materials over the Internet. In response, SunnComm Technologies came up with a copy guard system that would stop would-be computer pirates cold.

In the arms-race atmosphere of media conglomerates vs. file-traders, sooner or later some brilliant hacker would crack the program.

Well, it turned out to be sooner- quite a bit sooner- almost immediately, in fact. When confronted with the new copy protection, a student from Princeton figured out a way around the sophisticated system- simply hold down the "shift" key- a trick he shared with the world- via the Internet.

(POLITICAL CAMPAIGN CATEGORY)

Excerpt from the Bush-Mondale debate:

Walter Mondale: George Bush doesn't have the manhood to apologize.

Bush: Well, on the manhood thing, I'll put mine up against his any time.

(HEADLINE CATEGORY)

The *L.A. Times* printed a story about a rush of legislation the mayor was signing into law. The Headline was supposed to read "Mayor's Pen Is Busiest In Town". We'll leave it to you to figure out which space was omitted.

(VACUOUS CATEGORY)

Supermodel Beverly Johnson added a new wrinkle in the war on poverty when she declared "Everyone should have enough money to get plastic surgery." That should give all the poor folk a lift.

(FAMOUS LAST WORDS CATEGORY)

During the Civil War, Union General John Sedgwick dismissed warnings from his concerned men to take cover during the Battle of Spotsylvania Court House with, "They couldn't hit an elephant at this dist…." General Sedgwick was missed by his troops, his family and his friends- but apparently not by enemy snipers.

(LOWERED EXPECTATIONS CATEGORY)

A bank in Marked Tree, Arkansas, was broken into but after the thief found all the money locked securely away, he contented himself with a clock radio and a box full of candies. Even though security cameras caught everything, he still might have gotten away with it had he not been a litter bug as well, leaving a trail of candy wrappers for police to follow right to his door. The irony is that the candies were Dum Dums.

(PETTY THEFT CATEGORY)

In a crime the Fresno County Sheriff's Department characterized as "Pure genius", a car thief broke into a car and managed to lock himself in the trunk. When police arrived, following a trail of blood to the locked trunk from another car which had been burglarized, they expected to find a victim. Instead they discovered the crook trapped in the trunk along with his ill-gotten gain. Seems he had cut himself breaking into the other car. The police had their man who was read his rights and no doubt advised to find another line of work.

(NEW PRODUCT CATEGORY)

Microsoft, UK, issued a press release touting their new ILoo, an Internet-ready toilet with a broadband connection, waterproof keyboard, plasma screen and special sponsored toilet paper loaded with web addresses. Resisting the temptation of using any crude references to "downloading" in their sales materials, the company chose instead to boast that the ILoo would allow "instant logging on."

Twelve days later, after the country had made the ILoo a laughingstock, renaming it the "ILulu", damage control hacks at Microsoft issued a statement claiming that it had all been an April Fools joke. Problem was, the original press release was issued on April 30th- a bit late for April Fools.

Nobody bought the Microsoft Merry Pranksters story and the company finally had to admit that it wasn't a joke- it was a real product which, upon further reflection, they had decided not to release after all.

(DOUBLESPEAK CATEGORY)

From Secretary Of Defense, Donald Rumsfeld: "Reports that say that something hasn't happened are always interesting to me, because as we know, there are known knowns; there are things we know we know. We also know there are known unknowns; that is to say we know there are some things we do not know. But there are also unknown unknowns — the ones we don't know we don't know."

WHAT'S UNCLE SAM HAVE IN HIS BELFRY?

Now it can be told. World War II's top secret, "Project X-Ray," was a weapon that would literally come at The Enemy like a "bat out of Hell".

The idea was to affix small napalm devices to hundreds of bats which were kept in a state of hibernation inside a large canister. Once dropped, the canister, slowed by a parachute, would open, the bats would disperse, head for enemy buildings and... well after this point you can imagine that it wasn't pleasant for either the bats or The Enemy. Let's just say that the bats wouldn't have to worry about collecting their military pensions.

Think it was crazy? You say it wouldn't work? Well, the scientists behind the project proved that it would. During one test, a couple of the bats woke up early, flew off and managed to burn the brand new Carlsbad Auxiliary Army Air Base in New Mexico to the ground. Maybe they should have named it "The Man-Bat-tin Project".

BATHROOM BLOOPER-
BECAUSE IT'S... EVERYWHERE!

Even if they are in great shape, mountain climbers scaling Mount McKinley in Alaska are getting pooped- literally. The state has strict regulations about personal waste disposal way up there on the roof of North America but they suspect that many climbers are, shall we say, claiming squatter's rights anywhere they see fit. While officially, solid waste is to be carried off the mountain or dropped down a crevasse, enough is being scattered willy-nilly that about a third of climbers who go up, come down with gastroenteritis- a condition that is brought about by poor waste management and the nearly immediate results of which further contribute to the problem. Health officials advise anyone scaling the peak to boil all drinking water made from melted snow.

UNFRIENDLY SKIES

Back in the good old days when the only security issue airline passengers had to sweat was skyjacking, one US airline hired two psychiatrists to mingle with and quietly screen the passengers for any sign of nervousness or evil intent that might betray a skyjacker. Each shrink was hired separately and worked unbeknownst to the other.

Sure enough, by the end of the first day, after screening hundreds of passengers, the scheme paid off with a likely suspect. One psychiatrist had the other one arrested.

NOT EVERYBODY
CAN BE A COPYWRITER

*Bloopers and blunders are nothing new-
just consider these beauties from the days of classic radio:*

Announcer: "When you are thirsty, try 7-Up, the refreshing drink in the green bottle with the big 7 on it and u-p after."
Another gem along the same lines was the introduction of popular banjo player Eddy Peabody:
Announcer: "And now Mr. Eddy Playbody will pee for you."

NOT EVERYBODY
CAN BE A TALENT SCOUT

Another old-time classic blunder came when a studio executive noted on Fred Astaire's first screen-test, "Can't act. Can't sing. Can dance a little."

UNLUCKY STRIKE

A Pennsylvania man got some serious burns in some serious places when he decided to catch a smoke in a portable toilet he was using. As soon as he lit up, a tremendous explosion demolished the potty. The man can't recall whether he was launched or jumped out but he did remember to call a lawyer and file suit against the company providing the convenience. The $10 million dollar claim contends that there should have been a "No Smoking" sign on the door as the toilet was located over buried methane lines.

THE BAD SEED

New Zealand's South island is one of the most beautiful spots in the world but teens everywhere grow bored easily and a certain group of adolescents decided on some mischief to spice up their lives. They went to a local seed company and decided to cut the zip ties holding the door of a shipping container closed. What were they expecting to find? Probably not the several tons of peas which instantly engulfed them, that's for sure. One boy was trapped under the mountain of peas and had to be rescued by forklift. The defendants were sentenced to community service, ordered to pay restitution for the damaged seeds and reminded to henceforth mind their peas and q's.

HE STARTED AS CLYDE BUT ALMOST ENDED UP BONNIE

With the exception of jewel thief, being a bank robber is the most glamorous life of crime. It draws criminal wannabes of all types. Take the young man who held up National City Bank in Columbus, Ohio, for example. He managed to pull off the theft but had a bit of trouble with the getaway. Apparently new at the game, he stuffed the huge bundle of cash down his pants and made a run for it. He was unaware that banks often slip in a small explosive device loaded with purple dye to mark the bills which detonates a short while after the robber leaves the bank. When the charge went off, something else nearly did as well. The term "Purple Passion" now has a whole new meaning to this crook.

PLENTY OF PENNIES
BUT NO SENSE

In Rhode Island, a 33 year-old crook knocked over an armored car by knocking out the driver. He grabbed four bags containing $800 each and made his getaway- err, really more of a crawl-away. The bags each contained $800 in pennies. The cops caught up to him so fast they could have stopped for a nice doughnut en route.

ET, PHONE YOUR
INSURANCE COMPANY

An emergency room in Aracruz, Brazil, went on alert after locals reported seeing a fireball and witnessing a badly burned alien fall out of the sky. When the patient arrived, doctors set right to work but despite their best efforts, "ET" was doomed to forever remain a burnt rubber doll. Police chalked it up as a practical joke.

A CURRENT AFFAIR

Pity the poor housewife who came home to find her husband in the kitchen quivering frantically at the end of a wire that seemed to be tethered to an electric appliance. Reacting instantly, she dashed out the back door, picked up a stray board and used it to pound her husband away from the deadly current. She broke hubby's arm in two places but it was worth it- she had saved him from death by Walkman.

MEDICAL MUCK-UPS

The following notes were written by doctors
and gleaned from patients' charts.
It just goes to show that if laughter is the best medicine,
some MD's are liable to give you an overdose.

"Patient has chest pain if she lies on her left side for over a year."

"The patient was to have a bowel resection. However, he took a job as a stockbroker instead."

"On the 2nd day the knee was better and on the 3rd day it disappeared completely."

"She is numb from her toes down."

"The patient has been depressed ever since she began seeing me in 1993."

"The patient refused an autopsy."

"The patient has no past history of suicides."

"She stated that she had been constipated for most of her life, until she got a divorce."

"While in the ER, she was examined, X-rated and sent home."

"Many years ago the patient had frostbite of the right shoe."

"She slipped on the ice and apparently her legs went in separate directions in early December."

"The patient was in his usual state of good health until his airplane ran out of gas and crashed."

"Patient has left his white blood cells at another hospital."

"Patient was released to outpatient department without dressing."

"The lab test indicated abnormal lover function."

A TOUGH WAY TO SAVE A DIME

A couple of French felons hatched a plot to rob a bank by tunneling through a wall in the building next door. They worked long into the night but brick by brick they drew ever nearer their goal. Finally, in the wee small hours, they triumphantly broke into the bank. Unfortunately, they found themselves in the bathroom. The vault? They missed it completely.

UP IN THE AIR

Many people say that parachuting is dangerous. Even more would insist that you shouldn't do it with a medical condition. Just about everyone can agree that you shouldn't jump out of a plane if you are near full term in your pregnancy. Everyone, apparently, except a young Russian sky diving enthusiast, who found herself in labor thousands of feet up in freefall. Although she almost passed out several times, the woman managed to "hold on," if you'll excuse the expression, until she landed, whereupon she immediately gave birth. Wonder if she named the kid "Geronimo!"?

FOR WHOM THE CELL TOLLS

In Anniston, Alabama, a man led police on a merry chase for hours after being ordered to pull his motorcycle over for a traffic violation. He finally ditched the bike and sprinted into deep woods where the cops couldn't track him but just as they were about to give up, the guy's cell phone rang, betraying his hiding spot 50 feet up a tree. Now he's got a cell to go with his cell phone.

HALF-HEARTED HOLDUP

A fast-food joint in Ypsilanti, Michigan, was held up a few years back by a man who flashed a gun and demanded money. The guy behind the counter explained that he couldn't open the cash register without a food order so the holdup man checked the menu and ordered onion rings. The employee pointed out that onion rings were not available at breakfast time so the would-be thief became discouraged and left without any money- or onion rings.

ONE FOR THE ROAD

An Arkansas man who had the good sense to call for a designated driver when he was too tipsy to operate a car should have also called for a designated rider. The 38 year-old man jumped out the window of the car at an estimated 60 m.p.h while going after his cigarette which had been sucked out. We'd like to think that he was simply concerned about litter or the chance of a forest fire rather than just being a drunken, cheap, nicotine freak.

A LOVER'S SPATTER

A nineteen year old woman was arrested for pouring boiling oil over her boyfriend in Eugene, Oregon. The reason? They had gotten into an argument over a Bible passage they had been reading together. Perhaps someone needs to step back and take a look at the bigger message here.

SPOILSPORTS

A campaign to stop kite-flying on the grounds of the Washington Monument was cooked up by the Park Police in 1970. They cited a law written by Congress to keep the Wright Brothers' planes from getting fouled in the kite strings. Guess back then, as the 60's were winding down, there were enough people higher than a kite already.

"CRIMINAL LAWYER"-
ISN'T THAT REDUNDANT?

In Tulsa, Oklahoma, one Marshall Cummings decided he didn't need a lawyer to defend him at his upcoming trial. He'd seen enough "Perry Mason" episodes on TV to know how things go. Marshall was confident that he could exonerate himself. Then he got his chance. Confronting his accuser in court, he fixed her with a steely Raymond Burr style stare and asked "Did you get a good look at my face when I took your purse?" Case closed. Cummings was given ten years to bone up on the fine points of being a criminal lawyer.

SPORTS SNORTS

"Baseball is ninety percent mental. The other half is physical."
-Yogi Berra

"They X-Rayed my head and found nothing."
-Jerome "Dizzy" Dean

"All I had to do is keep turning left!"
-George Robson, on how he won the 1946 Indy 500

"Me and George and Billy are two of a kind."
-Mickey Rivers, of the Texas Rangers, commenting on his cordial relationship with Yankee owner Steinbrenner and manager Billy Martin

"I don't know. I'm not in shape yet."
-Yogi Berra, when asked his cap size

"A lot of good ballgames on tomorrow, but we're going to be right here with the Cubs and the Mets."
-Thom Brennaman, Chicago Cubs broadcaster

"Sure, there have been deaths and injuries in boxing, but none of them serious."
-Alan Winter

"We have only one person to blame, and that's each other."
-Barry Beck, New York Ranger, on who started a brawl during the Stanley Cup playoffs

"Fans, don't fail to miss tomorrow's game."
        -*"Dizzy Dean", baseball great turned sports announcer*

"It's almost like we have ESPN."
        -*Magic Johnson, on how well he and James Worthy*
        work together

"You've got to be very careful if you don't know where you're going, because you might not get there."
        -*Yogi Berra*

"I wouldn't ever set out to hurt anyone deliberately unless it was, you know, important-like a league game or something."
        -*Dick Butkus*

"I don't know. They had bags over their heads."
        -*Yogi Berra, when asked if the streakers who dashed*
        across the field naked were men or women.

"I can't really remember the names of the clubs that we went to."
        -*Shaquille O'Neal, answering whether he had*
        visited the Parthenon while in Greece.

"Even Napoleon had his Watergate."
        -*Danny Ozark, Philadelphia Phillies manager,*
        commenting on the Phillies' ten-game losing streak

"It's tough to make predictions- especially about the future."
        -*Yogi Berra*

"The similarities between me and my father are different."
        -*Dale Berra, Yogi Berra's son*

GRAMBO

A sweet, blue-haired old granny had completed a pleasant day of shopping at the mall and was tottering back to her car when she noticed four strange men lurking in her vehicle. Like any normal old lady, she immediately dropped her shopping bags and drew her gun, threatening to open fire if the mangy varmints didn't make tracks. The frightened men complied and took off, as Granny might have put it, like the dickens.

Puzzled as to why the key wouldn't fit, the pistol-packin' Grandma noticed an identical car a few spaces down and realized that sure enough, that other auto was her car. The contrite woman then drove to the police station and reported the incident. When she came in, four men already at the counter cowered in her presence. They were there ahead of her, reporting that they were car-jacked by a mean old lady. No charges were filed and it was just as well- the cops were laughing too hard to do any paperwork.

SMOKE SCREEN

Back in the fifties, a cigarette was marketed as being "Mild as May." Going after the female market with a vengeance, Philip Morris even outfitted their new brand with red filter so that lipstick wouldn't show up against it. In this instance at least, women were too smart to fall for it- but men weren't. The company simply doffed the colored filters, slapped a rough-hewn cowboy image on the brand and created one of the top-selling cigarettes even to this day- Marlboro. Wonder if the Marlboro Man has any idea he's puffing on a coffin-nail originally made for the ladies?

AND THEY WONDER WHY THE MAIL IS SO SLOW

In 1999, the good old United States Postal Service printed a batch of international stamps featuring our national pride and joy: the Grand Canyon. Each stamp was emblazoned with this message: "Grand Canyon, Colorado." One small problem- the Grand Canyon is located in Arizona.

HELLO DELI

Down in Miami, a crook tried to rob a delicatessen but the owner was ready for him with a three-foot salami. He let the thief have it right in the face which broke his nose and no doubt made his eyes water. The holdup man ran for it and took refuge in the trunk of a car- one that just happened to belong to undercover cops. (Some days it just doesn't pay to get out of bed.) The crook was finally arrested five days later when the cops heard whimpers coming from their trunk.

BATHROOM BLOOPER- ENOUGH TO MAKE YOU FLIP YOUR LID

A Chicago woman tottered to the bathroom early one morning and sleepily glanced at the toilet before she used it. What she saw opened her eyes in a snap-the bowl was inhabited by a sizeable snake. Lucky she looked first- lucky for both the woman and the snake. Animal control officers opined that it had slithered in through the pipes. Either that or it was the absolute final reminder to pay her plumbing bill.

TAKING A POWDER

Victoria, Australia, police drug dogs were well-trained but never seemed to find any drugs. After a thorough investigation, the Australian police got to the bottom of the situation. All seven members of the sniff squad were trained on talcum powder. The dogs were taken off duty until they could be retrained.

ORANGE HAIR WOULD HAVE BEEN A NICE TOUCH, TOO

When crooks go to jail, they often learn tips and tricks of the trade from their cellmates. A few pointers that the cellmates of two ex-bank robbers from Corinth, Maine, will probably pick up are:

A: don't make your getaway in full sight of dozens of witnesses

B: don't use a purple pick-up truck as your getaway vehicle and

C: if you must use a purple pick-up truck, try to find one without flames painted down the sides.

PRACTICE MAKES PERFECT

An attempted robbery at the 7-Eleven store in Mishawaka, Indiana, was foiled after one of the robbers gave the clerk a note demanding that she "put it in the bag." After the clerk explained that she didn't understand what the note said, the robber snatched back the paper and had to admit that he didn't either- his accomplice had written it. This led to an argument between the two men who subsequently decided to call off the heist and run for it.

LOST IN TRANSLATION

Here are a few classic product names, slogans and other phrases which are fine in their original language but run into trouble when translated into foreign tongues:

"Pepsi brings your ancestors back from the grave."
- *"Pepsi Comes Alive" as originally translated into Chinese*

"Bite the wax tadpole."
- *Coca-Cola's mangled name in Chinese*

The Chinese translation of KFC's "finger lickin' good" was also problematical. It was translated as "eat your fingers off."

When it came to reliability, the Chevy Nova was one of the great American cars. It was very popular for many years in the US but when Chevy set up shop in South America, they found that their shiny little American dreams weren't selling. They learned why after an expensive ad campaign bombed. In Spanish, "no va" means "doesn't go".

"You are invited to take advantage of the chambermaid."
-From a guest directory at a Japanese hotel.

"Got Milk?" is a huge success in the US but when the Dairy Association went south of the border, it was translated as "Are you lactating?"

"I am a jelly doughnut."
- *Translation of John F. Kennedy's famous Berlin speech*

"It takes a virile man to make a chicken pregnant."
-Perdue chicken ad, as mistranslated overseas

When in Bangkok, be sure to visit the cleaners which goes after English-speaking customers with the sign: "Drop your trousers here for best results."

Coors came up with the catchy slogan "Turn It Loose" but when they turned it loose in Spanish, they were trying to sell beer with the pitch, "Suffer From Diarrhea."

And one of the best, found on a sign in an Acapulco hotel: "The manager has personally passed all the water served here."

FOUR FLUSH FOLLY SALUTES: THE BEST OF THE WORST

(PUBLIC SERVICE MESSAGE CATEGORY)

In New York, an anti-drug group decided to get the lead out in their "Too Cool To Do Drugs" campaign. How better to get the message across to school kids than to hand out free pencils with the slogan emblazoned on them? The pencils were distributed but as the pencils were used, a problem arose. After the first sharpening, the message read "Cool To Do Drugs" and eventually the pencils just said "Do Drugs."

(CAREER CHOICES CATEGORY)

Tough-guy actor George Raft was left with some hard-boiled egg on his face after some bad career moves during the 0's. First, he turned down the lead in the classic *High Sierra*, part that went to Humphrey Bogart. Then he turned down the lead in the classic *The Maltese Falcon*, a part that went to Humphrey Bogart. He followed that brilliant move with declining the role of Rick in the classic *Casablanca*, a part that went to Humphrey Bogart. Finally, Raft topped off these blunders by turning down the lead in the classic *Double Indemnity*, a part that went to Humph....err, Fred MacMurray.

(BROADCASTING CATEGORY)

The President of CBS reportedly reacted incredulously with "Preempt Doris Day? Are you out of your mind?" Thus, CBS declined *Monday Night Football*, a franchise that has racked up billions in ad revenues ever since for ABC.

(GAME SHOW CATEGORY)

You're In the Picture, a 1961 game show hosted by Jackie Gleason, lasted all of one airing. The next week, Gleason appeared and spent the half hour apologizing for the horrendous program of the previous week

NO FLY LIST

When Homeland Security authorities determined that the names "Nelson" and "David" might be used by terrorists, they put out word and sure enough bagged David Nelson, Ozzie and Harriet's eldest son. Nelson, who grew up on radio and TV as a member of one of America's most beloved families, was stopped from boarding his flight at John Wayne Airport. His nefarious scheme? Going to visit his daughter in Salt Lake City. Another dangerous threat to airline security, Senator Edward Kennedy, also found himself stopped from boarding a plane to Boston from Washington DC. Even with all his connections and a full Senate staff, it took him several weeks to get off the list.

BATHROOM BLOOPER- ON THE POT AND ON THE CLOCK

Some employers are now using a new generation of productivity tools including an ID card with a magnetic strip to track how many times an employee has used the bathroom. Another item is a stall that does a urine drug test automatically, and, the crown jewel of the throne room, stall doors which fling open wide after a preset interval, whether the person occupying the stall is finished or not.

AND YOU THOUGHT RECEPTIONS WITH AN OPEN BAR WERE BAD...

An old Serbian custom involves the groom shooting an apple at his wedding. It's supposed to be done carefully and with a pistol. One groom however, a police marksman, decided to kick it up a notch and use a shotgun instead. He succeeded in making applesauce but also hit fifteen guests, causing minor wounds. The embarrassed groom spent his wedding night in jail instead of with his bride.

HIS NICKNAME WAS "CHICKEN TERIYAKI"

Kamikaze pilots of World War II were supposed to go on one-way missions but one pilot made no less than eleven round-trip suicide flights. He returned safely every time and lived to the ripe old age of 93. In his autobiography, he grumbled that he considered the kamikaze planes "unsafe."

ALL AT SEA

A civic-minded citizen wanted to help the Coast Guard so he set out to raise money by windsurfing from North Devon to Lundy Island. When he failed to show up at the appointed time, a massive air-sea rescue was mounted using ferries, a helicopter, lifeboats, a mobile coast guard unit and dozens of personnel. The windsurfer was found and the rescue cost twice the amount he had raised for the Coast Guard fund.

SECRET AGENT BUGS BUNNY

During World War II, the OSS, the organization that would later become the CIA, commissioned a study of Hitler's health. They determined that Der Fuhrer was near the male-female line and that it wouldn't take much to push him over. With no mustache and a high-pitched voice, Hitler would lose credibility among his people they reasoned. So with the greatest secrecy, they bribed his gardener to inject estrogen in Hitler's carrots. For a few extra Deutschmarks, maybe they could have had arsenic injected instead.

A FOOL AND HIS MONEY...

Ever feel dumb for making a bad investment? Cheer up-you're in good company. Mark Twain, one of the sharpest knives ever to be found in any drawer, once declined a chance to invest in a newfangled invention and instead sunk his dough in a new typesetting machine. The company went broke and Twain was hornswoggled. The chance he turned down? Alexander Graham Bell's nifty little gadget, the telephone.

AN ALARMING CRIME

Two British teens looking for kicks decided to break into a grocery store. The inexperienced duo spotted what they thought was the cash box on the wall, pried if off and ran for it. The box began buzzing and howling so they threw it to the ground and stomped on it to quiet it down. Nonetheless, it just kept getting louder and as they ran in desperation, they finally tossed it in the river. It turns out the pimply-faced perpetrators stole the store's burglar alarm instead of the cash box.

SOMETHING FISHY

A woman returning from a trip to Singapore aroused the suspicions of Melbourne, Australia, customs officials after they heard "flipping noises" coming from beneath her skirt. A natural reaction to airline food? Possibly, but the continued thrashing prompted agents to take a closer look. That's when they discovered 51 live tropical fish happily swimming around in an apron of water-filled plastic bags. The moral is, if you want to smuggle fish into Australia, you've got to keep them quiet- maybe Jell-O in their bags?

IN RELATED NEWS...

In Prague, a man was caught smuggling rare animals. Believe it or not, it wasn't the snake he had stashed in his pants that gave him away. It was a search of his luggage which contained turtles, scorpions and a horned viper. In all, they seized 60 live animals.

FROSTY RECEPTION

Sir Winston Churchill was famed for his wit, his stubbornness and his capacity for putting in long hours of hard work but even he had his off days. It was on one of those days that he threw his support to a scheme to build fast cheap aircraft carriers out of ice. Churchill put Lord Montbatten in charge of the project. He, in turn, worked with American scientists who discovered that mixing a little wood pulp in with the water before freezing made an extremely tough material. Taking a block of the stuff to a conference in 1943, Montbatten wanted to demonstrate how enemy torpedoes would simply bounce off and fired a gun at the block. As predicted, the bullet ricocheted- right into a nearby officer. The officer recovered but the idea was put on ice permanently.

BEWARE OF STRANGERS WITH CANDY

A woman in Lexington, Kentucky, was understandably overjoyed to win a local radio station's "100 Grand" contest. She had spent hours listening and then dialing in at just the right time to be the lucky 10th caller. When she stopped by the station the next day to pick up her prize, she was asked to return later. Upon arriving home, she had a phone message from the general manager that explained she had, in fact, won a Nestle 100 Grand candy bar and not actual money. The judge will decide if she is to ultimately win sweet revenge.

THE HOUSEGUESTS FROM HADES

You've heard the old adage from Ben Franklin about fish and visitors but a 46 year-old Illinois man took things to extremes. He had been enduring a couple of unwelcome houseguests who simply refused to leave. Despite his hints, suggestions, pleadings and demands, they still remained. Finally, his insistence turned to threats and eventually escalated to an ultimatum: "Get out or I'll burn down the house." They didn't so he did, dousing everything with alcohol and touching it off with a lighter. The two-story home was engulfed in flames so the guests finally took the hint and left- unharmed. The poor, frazzled host was charged with arson and given municipal accommodations.

ANOTHER WASHINGTON COVER UP

Former Attorney General John Ashcroft ordered that two statues in the ceremonial Great Hall of the Justice Department be covered up with blue drapes because they were too scantily clad. The female "Spirit of Justice" and the male "Majesty of Law" had stood in the hall since the 1930's but were deemed too racy for Ashcroft's tenure and $8,000 of your tax dollars were spent to provide the artworks some modesty. Ashcroft's successor spent several months agonizing over the issue but in the end decided to dare to go bare.

TO BE A SUCCESSFUL THIEF, YOU NEED THE RIGHT SHOES

A thief broke into a car in Bergen, Norway, and stole a case containing 25 shoes. Not 25 pairs of shoes, just 25 left shoes. The case belonged to a shoe salesman and as they were pretty difficult to fence unless Imelda Marcos happens to lose her right leg, the thief tossed his booty away in disgust.

IT'S NOT NICE TO FOOL MOTHER NATURE

In the late 1950's, oceanfront residents of a small, seaside town in New Jersey got the notion that both their lives and property values would be enhanced if they got rid of the pesky sand dunes that obscured their views of the Atlantic. With them gone, they could gaze out upon the ocean in all its panoramic splendor. In came the bulldozers and out went the stately dunes which had safeguarded the shore for hundreds of years. The oceanfront property owners were right, for they gained a spectacular view, particularly of the 15 foot waves cascading atop a 12 foot storm surge that crashed through their picture windows a short time later. The Great March Storm of 1962 was one of the biggest things ever to hit the Jersey Shore. It devastated a huge swath of shoreline. The damage was mitigated only by the massive dunes which provided a natural barrier to the elements-except in the aforementioned hapless community.

MAKING PIZZA DOUGH THE HARD WAY

A Las Vegas man decided to shift career tracks right in the middle of his job application at a local pizza joint. He suddenly pulled a gun and demanded his severance pay from the cash register before he was even hired. The frightened clerk handed over $200 and the job applicant took off. Just so you know, the guy got a callback on his application- from the police, who were very impressed that he used his real name and address.

IT CAME FROM SNAPPLE

In monster movies, New York has been besieged by both towering dinosaurs and rogue aliens but a promotion by Snapple resulted in a new horror, "The Attack Of The 25 Foot Popsicle." The seventeen and a half ton Kiwi-Strawberry frozen confection was to have set a world's record but instead, temperatures on the first day of Manhattan's summer caused sudden and catastrophic melting before it could be hoisted into place. Like something out of *Ghostbusters*, the resulting wave of sugary Kiwi-Strawberry goo engulfed Union Square and caused some minor accidents as the 35,000 pounds of slush coated every surface in the vicinity and sent onlookers clambering for higher ground. Streets were shut down and traffic was diverted while "Popzilla" was battled with fire hoses until finally retreating down the sewer. One can only wonder what's next- "The Attack Of The Kiwi-Strawberry Alligator"?

NEXT SEASON'S HOT NEW REALITY SHOW

In the decadent days of the Roman Empire, they warmed up the audience for the gladiators with the spectacle of unarmed men being hunted and cut down by armed fighters. As the crowd roared approval, the victor's weapons were taken away and he became the next victim. Hard to believe they got a lot of volunteers.

UNSAFE CRACKERS

In 1987, Danish bank robbers used dynamite to try to open a safe. The first five times, using ever increasing amounts of dynamite, it didn't work. On the sixth attempt, they really piled on the explosives. That blast didn't open the safe either but they did manage to blow up the bank and produce a boom heard miles away.

YOUR TAX DOLLARS AT SHIRK

Multnomah County, Oregon, is looking for a few good Klingons. Actually, one human who is fluent in Klingon will do, thank you. The county Department of Human Services, which serves about 60,000 mental health clients, is searching for an English-Klingon interpreter for those Trekkies and Trekkers who have gone 'round the bend to where no man has gone before and will only communicate in Klingon. The Portland area's cosmopolitan mix of cultures obligates the county to provide interpreters in all foreign languages.

MESSAGE FROM SPACE SHEEPISHLY DENIED

Intelligence analysts in Cheltenham, England, almost had the wool pulled over their eyes by a strange signal emanating from a Yorkshire signal station. The high frequency signals only occurred in the daytime and were initially attributed to aliens. Upon further investigation, intelligence officials discovered that the signal was produced by a ram rubbing his head against the antenna between his daily frolics with the local ewes. Maybe it was his way of bragging.

KANSAS JUSTICE

When a man was found guilty of robbery and kidnapping, a Kansas jury sentenced him to 5005 years in prison. The judge ruled that that was an unacceptly long sentence and reduced it to 1001 years. Maybe if the convict is lucky, he'll get a couple centuries off for good behavior.

UP TO THEIR NECKS IN IT

Thrilled that they had been honored with permission to be the first ever to explore Great Britain's most inaccessible loch, the West Country Sub-Aqua Club set their sights on exploring the underwater world of the remotest Scotland. The team drove 740 miles, climbed 3000 feet and donned elaborate underwater gear in preparation for the dive. What would they discover in the cold, dark depths of the unknown? It wasn't long until they made their first major discovery- the loch was only four feet deep.

ONE FOR THE BOOKS

Swedish business consultant Ulf af Trolle sunk thirteen years of effort into writing his book. Thirteen years of painstaking research, writing, rewriting, editing, indexing and more rewriting. He took the 250 page manuscript to an office center to be copied and a cheerful clerk dropped it in the copier- oops, sorry- that was the shredder. Ouch!

CHAIN OF EVIDENCE

A couple of crooks got the idea of robbing a cash machine in Kentucky by hooking a chain from the front of the machine to the bumper of their pickup truck. They then gave it the gas but instead of the front being pulled off the auto teller, the bumper was ripped off their truck. With this turn of events, they panicked and drove away leaving the chain attached to the ATM, the bumper attached to the chain and their license plate attached to the bumper.

THE BEER HAS A BETTER HEAD THAN HE DOES

An Arkansas man with a powerful thirst had a hankering for beer. Rather than go through the usual procedure, he decided to pick up a handy cinderblock and toss it through the liquor store window. He let her fly with a heave-ho and only then discovered that the window was made of Plexiglas. The cinder block bounced back and knocked him unconscious. He was even provided a souvenir of the whole incident courtesy of the security camera videotape.

STING BIKINI

A former Miss St. Tropez accidentally stepped on a bee hive. No that's not dumb, just unfortunate. When she showed up at the beach covered in bandages, eager imitators made bikinis from bandages and medical gauze. This inaugurated the "medical look" fashion that swept the beach that season. Now that's really dumb.

SELF HELP

Readers of *Self* magazine who suffer from dry mouth benefited from this expert advice to manage the condition: "take frequent sips of water." Thank goodness we have science to watch out for us.

OVER THE FALLS

Niagara Falls is famous for two things: honeymoons and going over the falls in a barrel. Both involve a lot of faith and a high degree of danger. Now there is a third, slightly crazier, thing to add to the "taking the plunge" list: going over the falls without a barrel. A 40 year-old Michigan man who had been drinking, took the leap in nothing but his street clothes. He survived the fall and made it back to shore only to be arrested. The Park Police take that sort of thing seriously. The judge took it even more seriously: he fined the man $5,000 (Canadian) and barred the daredevil from the Canadian Falls for life. On the plus side, the fame got the guy a $100,000 contract with a circus.

MORE BLOOPER BRIEFS

A Scotts Valley, California, father was arrested for leaving his toddler alone in an SUV for 45 minutes in a mall parking lot. While his child was in the vehicle, Dad was sitting in a restaurant taking part in a Bible study group.

This correction appeared in a Warrenton, Virginia, newspaper: "Important notice: If you are one of the hundreds of parachuting enthusiasts who bought our 'Easy Sky Diving' book, please make the following correction : On page 8, line 7, the words 'state zip code' should have read 'pull rip cord.'"

Actor James Earl Jones was once honored with a plaque which should have read: "Thank you, James Earl Jones, for keeping the dream alive." The engraver made a mistake and, instead, the name read "James Earl Ray", the man who was convicted of assassinating Martin Luther King, Jr.

"Everything that can be invented has been invented."
-Commissioner of the U.S. Office of Patents,
Charles Duell, in 1899

"Louis Pasteur's theory of germs is a ridiculous fiction."
-French physiology professor Pierre Pachet, in 1872

"You've done a nice job of decorating the White House."
*-Singer Jessica Simpson, complimenting
Secretary of the Interior, Gale Norton, while
touring the White House*

"I think there is a world market for maybe five computers."
-IBM chairman Thomas Watson, in 1943

Warren Austin, representing the U.S. in the United Nations in 1948, said that to quell conflicts in the Middle East, Jews and Arabs should settle their differences "like good Christians."

Henri Matisse's masterpiece, "Le Bateau", was hung upside down for 47 days during its 1961 exhibition at New York's Museum of Modern Art.

LET THE PUNISHMENT FIT THE FINE

A Texas man was convicted of robbery and given the choice of paying almost ten thousand dollars in damages or going to jail for two years. He chose to pay the money but then he tried to get away with handing over a forged check. The judge gave him his two years back plus eight more for the bad check. The moral is that, in Texas, it is bad to rob a citizen but really bad to cheat a judge.

HEAT OF BATTLE

British troops in Operation Desert Shield sweltered in camouflage uniforms ill-suited to the heat of the desert sun. They fricasseed in their fatigues simply because four years before, the British government sold its entire supply of cool desert uniform to the Iraquis.

JOB ASSESSMENT

The editor of the *San Francisco Examiner* fired Rudyard Kipling, telling him that he just didn't know how to use the English language.

IN IRVING WE TRUST?

One of the most embarrassing blunders ever in the publishing industry happened back in 1971. McGraw-Hill paid writer Clifford Irving a cool $500,000 advance for the autobiography of Howard Hughes, which Irving said he was writing in collaboration with the reclusive billionaire. He might have gotten away with it had Hughes not trimmed his fingernails enough to dial a phone and pronounce the whole thing a fraud. After extensive denials, Irving finally came clean and admitted the hoax. The publisher suffered further mortification when people began noticing the large sign on the famous McGraw-Hill building, erected by a financial institution that had leased their ground floor- "The Irving Trust Company".

WHITE HOUSE WHOPPERS

"Rarely is the question asked: Is our children learning?"
- *George W. Bush*

"One of the great things about books is sometimes there are some fantastic pictures."
- *George W. Bush*

"Nobody needs to tell me what I believe. But I do need somebody to tell me where Kosovo is."
- *George W. Bush*

"I'm the master of low expectations."
- *George W. Bush*

"It's clearly a budget. It's got numbers in it."
-*George W. Bush*

"It has been said by some cynic, maybe it was a former president, 'If you want a friend in Washington, get a dog.' Well, we took them literally – that advice, as you know. But I didn't need that because I have Barbara Bush."
-*George Bush*

"I just wanted to get a little attention."
-*George Bush, after vomiting on Japanese Prime Minister Kiichi Miyazawa*

"I have orders to be awakened at any time in the case of a national emergency, even if I'm in a cabinet meeting."
- *Ronald Reagan*

"Things are more like they are now than they ever were before."
    - Dwight D. Eisenhower

"I never drink coffee at lunch. I find it keeps me awake for the afternoon."
    -Ronald Reagan

"I've talked to you on a number of occasions about the economic problems our nation faces, and I am prepared to tell you it's in a hell of a mess – we're not connected to the press room yet, are we?"
    -Ronald Reagan

"Trees cause more pollution than automobiles."
    -Ronald Reagan

"I try not to commit a deliberate sin. I recognize that I'm going to do it anyhow because I'm human and I'm tempted. And Christ set some almost impossible standards for us. Christ said, 'I'll tell you that anyone who looks on a woman with lust in his heart has already committed adultery.' I've looked on a lot of women with lust. I've committed adultery in my heart many times."
    -Jimmy Carter in a Playboy *magazine interview in 1976*

"When the president does it, that means that it is not illegal."
    - Richard M. Nixon

"I would have made a good pope."
    -Richard M. Nixon

"This is a great day for France."
>   *-Richard M. Nixon, while attending the funeral*
>   *of Charles de Gaulle*

"I don't think you're going to see a great, great uproar in this country about the Republican committee trying to bug the Democratic headquarters."
>   *-Richard M. Nixon, four days after the*
>   *Watergate break-in*

"I strongly support the feeding of children."
>   *-Gerald Ford, discussing the School Lunch Bill*

"When more and more people are thrown out of work, unemployment results."
>   *-Calvin Coolidge*

WINDY CITY NOT WINDY ENOUGH TO BLOW AWAY TICKETS

Forget the Chicago Seven. Over a dozen motorists were issued parking tickets in Chicago after they legally parked along a street and went on their way. That's when the city came by and installed parking meters in front of the cars. In a true show of bureaucratic efficiency, a meter maid was on the scene within minutes to ticket the line of cars. Maybe they call it the "Second City" because if you stop any longer than that, they'll install a meter and give you a ticket.

HAPHAZARD HEADLINES-
IT MUST BE TRUE-
IT'S IN THE PAPER...

BUSH ORDERS ARMY TROOP TO U.S. VIRGINS

WAR DIMS HOPE FOR PEACE

(in a story about Los Angeles councilwoman Laura Chick)
CHICK ACCUSES SOME OF HER MALE
COLLEAGUES OF SEXISM

MAN STRUCK BY LIGHTNING
FACES BATTERY CHARGE

SAFETY EXPERTS SAY SCHOOL BUS PASSENGERS
SHOULD BE BELTED

BRITISH LEFT WAFFLES ON FALKLAND ISLANDS

STUD TIRES OUT

JUVENILE COURT TO TRY SHOOTING
DEFENDANT

PANDA MATING FAILS; VETERINARIAN TAKES OVER

REAGAN WINS ON BUDGET, BUT MORE LIES AHEAD

HOW TO WRITE AND SPEAK
LIKE A COLLEG GRADUATE

SQUAD HELPS DOG BITE VICTIM

TWO CONVICTS EVADE NOOSE, JURY HUNG

YOUTH HIT BY CAR RIDING BICYCLE

ILLITERACY IS STILL A POBLEM
AMONG MISSISSIPPI ADULTS

LOW PAY REASON FOR POVERTY, STUDY SAYS

STORM DELAYED BY BAD WEATHER

GRAVITY'S FASTBALL

It was a stunt calculated to bring joy to the hearts of baseball fans everywhere. It was 1939 and catcher Joe Sprintz was to catch the highest-flying ball ever at Treasure Island, site of San Francisco's World's Fair. Sprintz watched as a blimp hovering 1,000 feet overhead dropped a ball. He missed it. They dropped another- he missed it. Another try and that one too hit the ground as did number four. Finally, on the fifth attempt, Sprintz managed to get his glove under the ball, which he discovered was traveling at terminal velocity with a force as if it had been shot out of a cannon. The ball hit his glove and bent his arm down so much that when it snapped back, it knocked out four teeth. He dropped the ball, too.

LOVE IS A MANY SPLENDORED THING

A thirty-eight year-old South Carolina man was so smitten with love for his inamorata that he hired a helicopter to drop 10,000 love letters and 2500 carnations on the lawn of his former girlfriend. This overwhelming expression of undying love was answered with complete indifference. By that time, his dearly beloved had married another guy. What did the man get for his $3000 airborne valentine? A charge of littering.

ONLY IN NEW YORK

A man held up a Brooklyn bank for $2100 and made a clean getaway- from the bank guards maybe but not from the local muggers. The robber himself was held up before he could abscond with the loot. Infuriated, he reported the theft to the police who in turn arrested him.

MUMMY OR DUMMY?

It was all for a good cause so an Ohio high school physics teacher agreed to be duct taped to a wall as part of a fundraiser. Funny thing about duct tape though, since it's meant to keep heat in air ducts, it doesn't breathe. Just as the students were completing the taping process, the teacher's body superheated and he lost consciousness. His students realized what was happening and cut him free from his sticky situation, thereby saving his life and probably earning some extra credit towards their grades.

THEY'RE PLAYING OUR SONG

A pair of resourceful Australian composers used a computer to work out a hundred billion possible phone number dialing sequences and copyrighted the resulting tunes as their own. Every time someone uses a touch tone phone, musical notes are produced and in all likelihood, the composers own the legal right to the sequence. They compare it to patenting DNA sequences and insist that they intend to chase giant corporations for payment when their "music" is used.

FOWL SMELL

A village in Russia had to be evacuated after a local farmer took delivery of tons of chicken manure, which, along with heavy rain and hot weather, gave rise to millions upon millions of flies. Fifty homes had to be abandoned due to the massive cloud of insects and breathing in the area was only possible with the aid of a surgical mask. The farmer responsible reportedly has apologized to his neighbors for the entire chicken manure incident.

DOCTORS NO LONGER ON CALL

In Hong Kong, the local medical board found it necessary to ban cell phone use by doctors in operating rooms. They figured that the threat posed to patients outweighed the doctor's interest in following their stock investments or arranging a tee time. It should be noted that doctors resisted the rule and the board only moved on the issue after immense public pressure.

BATHROOM BLOOPER- YOU SHOULD HAVE THOUGHT OF THAT BEFORE WE STARTED THE CHAIN REACTION

A small nuclear reactor at the University of Florida in Gainesville had a slight design flaw. It was water-cooled and the building had lousy water pressure. A sign posted on the bathroom door warned not to use the toilet when the reactor was running. If the toilet was flushed, the reactor would immediately scram, setting off alarms all over the building. And you thought someone knocking on the door was annoying.

WOMAN ATTACKED BY VENDING MACHINE

A 73 year-old woman became trapped by a newspaper vending machine outside a large chain store outlet when her clothing got caught in the door. The woman was stuck for some time before someone went inside to the "courtesy" counter and told them of the old woman's plight. The store personnel refused to help, saying they weren't allowed to "tamper" with the vending machines. The woman was left trapped, bent over the machine for twenty minutes while an employee tried to call the newspaper office to send someone over. The old woman finally persuaded a store employee to drop two quarters in the slot so she could get free. The woman's daughter later stopped by the store and gave them a five dollar bill so that the next ten people who get stuck in the machine can be freed more quickly.

BATHROOM BLOOPER- A SLIGHT CASE OF GAS

A Hamden, Connecticut, man shuffled to the bathroom in the wee small hours of the morning to answer Nature's Call. The next call would be to 911. As the man switched on the light, the house exploded, rattling windows for blocks around. All five people in the house escaped without serious injury but the home was virtually demolished. Firefighters noted that the local utility company had been working on the gas mains in the area for about a week and it seems somehow the gas leaked into this hapless family's bathroom. When the light switch sparked, it turned the indoor plumbing into outdoor plumbing.

A VERY FUELISH DEED

With the situation in the world nowadays, nervousness about the future supply of gasoline is perfectly understandable but a family in Norfolk, England, took preparations for another energy crisis a bit too far. They decided to use their garage to stockpile 90 gallons of gas for a rainy day. That's dangerous enough, but even moreso was the fact that they used water cans to store the gas. The seals on the cans weren't up to the challenge of storing gasoline and so they leaked. And since the gas cans were stowed close to the furnace, when the temperature dropped...well, let's just say, things heated up real fast. The house went up in a fireball that could probably be seen from space but the lucky family survived. Who knows? They could now be living next door to you.

IN LIFE, WHEN ONE DOOR SHUTS, ANOTHER ALWAYS OPENS

In Detroit, an inept but dedicated burglar targeted a local hotel and worked his way up from the first to the seventh floor, trying 210 doors before he found one that had been left unlocked. He made his move and slipped into the darkened room- right into the arms of three very alert occupants- two cops and an FBI agent.

REACH OUT AND TOUCH SOMEONE

John Walter was fired from AT&T after only nine months in his job as president because it was felt that he lacked "intellectual leadership." His severance package amounted to $26 million- now who's intelligent and who isn't?

ROCKET SCIENCE

Great news for national security. The Pentagon has, at long last, conducted a successful test of an anti-missile missile. A missile launched from the West Coast was shot down over the Pacific by another missile fired from a small island. Detractors said it couldn't be done but the defense contractors proved them wrong using good old American ingenuity. In this case, that ingenuity involved tagging the target missile with a global positioning device to continually broadcast its precise position to the interceptor, a courtesy that any future enemy would presumably not provide.

WHEN DEALING WITH CONTRACTS ALWAYS READ THE FINE PRINT

Guns For Hire is an Arizona company which specializes in staging realistic gunfights for events and movies. One day, they got a call from a 47 year-old woman who spotted their ad and wanted to hire them to kill her husband. She got four years in jail and, presumably, a divorce.

FISHERMAN GETS A BITE

At Florida's Marathon Beach, a fisherman caught sight of a group of fins slicing the water just off shore. Responding to a lifelong dream of swimming with dolphins, he dove into the water, prepared for fun and frolic with Flipper. That's when he discovered that the fins weren't attached to playful dolphins but rather to hungry sharks. The man's buddies fished him out and the local hospital patched up his several missing chunks.

SKUNKED

In Palmer, Massachusetts, the fire department was called to extinguish a fire in a house trailer. It seems that the owner had been bothered by a family of skunks which lived under his home. His strategy was to smoke them out, so he dumped a load of gunpowder into his bathtub and then lit it. As they say, where's there's smoke, there's fire. Ultimately the plan worked, for the skunks were forced to find other accommodations—unfortunately, as the trailer was toast, so was its owner.

BEAM ME OUT SCOTTY

A British *Star Trek* fan spent about $11,000 to convert his one bedroom flat into the starship Enterprise. His décor features portholes, an infinity mirror in the ceiling, star fields and a command console. Not surprisingly, his wife left him for a slightly more earthbound mate.

IF YOU CAN'T BEAT 'EM, JOIN 'EM

It was a tense and dangerous situation in Oakland, California. Police had surrounded a gunman who had barricaded himself inside a house. The man withstood barrage after barrage of tear gas but still would not surrender. After nearly exhausting their arsenal of gas canisters, the police discovered that the man was standing next to them shouting to please come out and give himself up.

GUILTY CONSCIENCE

A manager for a California fast-food restaurant reported that he was robbed of about $300 after work. He sat down with the police sketch artist to describe the thief and after a very detailed description the artist came up with a sketch that looked remarkably like the victim. When the artist mentioned the resemblance, the man broke down and confessed that he had in fact taken the money himself. If the sound of a marker on paper was enough to break him down, wonder what would happen if he was given the third degree?

LEGAL LU-LUS

Democracy is a wonderful system. In what other form of government can an informed public carefully weigh all the issues and consider the qualifications of the field of candidates, then go to the polls and cast their votes for their chosen representatives who will then fan out to the various seats of government and proceed to pass totally idiotic laws? Here are just a few of the funniest...

Like that spicy Italian food? When indulging yourself in Indiana, keep in mind that within four hours of eating garlic, a person may not enter a movie house, theater, or ride a public streetcar.

Why did the chicken cross the road? In Georgia, it was just being a scofflaw. The Peach State actually made it illegal for poultry to perambulate across the street.

Anyone who has found that no good deed goes unpunished should vacation at White Mountain National Forest in New Hampshire. If you are caught hauling away trash, raking leaves, building a bench for the park or any other random act of kindness, you can be slapped with a $150 fine for "maintaining the national forest without a permit."

In Staten Island, New York, you may only water your lawn if the hose is held in your hand. What else would you hold it with?

In Fairbanks, Alaska, it is considered an offense to feed alcoholic beverages to a moose. Get Bullwinkle bombed, go to jail.

In Arizona, if you are attacked by a criminal or burglar, you are only allowed to protect yourself with the same weapon that the crook possesses. So if you live in Arizona and want to keep a gun in the house for protection, better keep one for the burglar too- no need to load it though.

In Carmel, New York, a man who appears in public while wearing a jacket and pants that do not match is not only tacky but committing a criminal act. Any citizen seeing a checkered jacket in the company of striped pants is urged to call the fashion police immediately.

Attending a concert in Greene, New York? Remember, it is illegal to eat peanuts and walk backwards on the sidewalks during a concert. That's something no one would want on their permanent record.

Best not be musical at all in New Hampshire, where a state law forbids foot tapping, head nodding or keeping time with music in any way in a tavern, restaurant or café. Drumming along with *Wipeout* would probably get you "the chair."

According to an Illinois state law, a man's female companion shall call him "master" while out on a date. The law does not apply to married couples in which case the wife can often be heard calling her husband something that sounds similar to "master."

Many religious folks talk about "Natural Law." Well, here's one that's about as unnatural as they get: in North Carolina, fights between cats and dogs are prohibited.

In Michigan it is legal for a robber to file a law suit, if he or she got hurt in your house. Better put in safety lighting around where you keep your silverware- oh, and railings for second-story men would be considerate as well.

North Dakota bars and restaurants are prohibited from serving beer and pretzels at the same time...Twisted logic at best.

In the unlikely event that you have one arm and decide to become a professional piano player- stay out of Iowa where the law requires you to play for free.

If you are convicted of driving while intoxicated in New Jersey, you are no longer eligible to apply for personalized license plates. So just forget any hope of getting "BOOZ-R", "TIE 1 ON","DUI" or "YBSOBER" on your bumper.

Another enlightened law in Oxford, Ohio, states that it is unlawful for a woman to appear in public while unshaven. This includes legs and face. Remember, Justice may be blind- but extremely well groomed.

In Louisiana it is illegal to rob a bank and then shoot at the bank teller with a water pistol. Does that mean the robber should use a real one instead?

In Oregon, it is against the law for a wedding ceremony to be performed at a skating rink. Obviously, it's just a way to keep the couple from getting cold feet.

MORE LABEL LUNACY

"Product will be hot after heating."
          -On a pudding package

"For indoor and outdoor use only."
          -On Chinese-made Christmas lights

"Caution: You must remove clothes before washing."
          -In a washing machine instruction book

"Warning: May contain nuts."
          -On a bag of peanuts

"Do not use for drying pets."
          -In a microwave oven manual

"Wearing of this garment does not enable you to fly."
          -On a Superman costume for kids

"Recycled flush water unsafe for drinking."
          -On a toilet at an Ann Arbor, Michigan,
          public sports facility

"Do not drive with sunshield in place."
          -On a dashboard sunshield

"Do not eat toner."
          -On a cartridge for a laser printer

"Do not use while sleeping."
  -On a hairdryer

"You could be a winner! No purchase necessary. Details inside."
  -On a bag of Frito chips

"Caution: The contents of this bottle should not be fed to fish."
  -On a dog shampoo bottle

"Remove wrapper, open mouth, insert muffin, eat."
  -Instruction on a muffin package

"Warning: May cause drowsiness."
  -On a Nytol sleep ad

"Not to be used for personal hygiene."
  -Warning on a toilet brush

"First, Carry to Fire."
  - Instructions on a fire extinguisher

NOT EXACTLY A DO-IT-YOURSELFER

King Phillip III, who ruled Spain in the seventeenth century, died from a fever induced by sitting too close to his fireplace for too long. He didn't move his chair away from the fire even though he was overheating because to do so was beneath him. Seems the royal chair mover had the night off.

REVENGE OF THE CATS

In the dark ages, the Church decided that cats were "ambassadors of the devil" and ordered that they be destroyed. For the next hundred years or so, the cat crusades exterminated millions of the purry ones, effectively wiping them out in Europe. While that certainly put Satan in his place, it had the unfortunate effect of triggering a population explosion among rats, which multiplied prodigiously in the absence of their primary predator. The widespread infestation of rats then led to the Black Plague and the rest is karmic history. Next time you see a kitty be extra nice.

THE HOLE-IN-THE-GROUND GANG

In England, a gang of thieves plotted to break into a warehouse filled with fireworks. Naturally, they chose to use a cutting torch to get through the door. When the flame broke through, it touched off a large crate by the door that contained the equivalent of a hundred pounds of gunpowder. The entire building then went up in a chain reaction. Amazingly, no one was hurt and the crooks took off into the well-illuminated night.

THE HEAT IS OFF

Back in 1912, the Howard Hotel was Baltimore's newest hostelry admired by one and all. When the workmen went to fire up the furnaces for heat they discovered a slight problem-the place had been built with no chimneys.

MASTERS OF MALAPROPS

"There is no reason anyone would want a computer in their home."

> *-Ken Olson, president, chairman and founder of Digital Equipment Corp., in 1977*

"Television won't matter in your lifetime or mine."

> *-Rex Lambert, in a 1936 editorial in* The Listener

"The Internet is a great way to get on the net."

> *-Former presidential candidate Bob Dole*

"Hark! I hear a white horse coming."

> *-From the old* Lone Ranger *radio program*

"I don't think anybody should write his autobiography until after he's dead."

> *-Movie mogul Samuel Goldwyn*

"It's no exaggeration to say the undecideds could go one way or the other."

> *-President George Bush, discussing voters during the 1988 presidential campaign*

"The atomic bomb will not go off. And I speak as an expert on explosives."

> *-Admiral W. Leahy to President Harry Truman, 1945*

"Outside of the killings, Washington has one of the lowest crime rates in the country."

> *- Marion Barry, Washington, D.C. Mayor*

"I haven't committed a crime. What I did was fail to comply with the law."

> *-Then New York City mayor David Dinkins, responding to accusations that he failed to pay his taxes*

"Every city I go to is an opportunity to paint, whether it's Omaha or Hawaii."

> *-Singer Tony Bennett*

"If there is one word to describe Atlantic City, it's Big Business. Or two words – Big Business."

> *-Donald Trump*

"Three-quarters of (the oil) was contained within the ship. There's been very little reporting on that."

> *-White House Chief of Staff John Sununu, speaking to the press after the Exxon Valdez spilled 250,000 barrels of oil into Alaska's Prince William Sound*

"The streets are safe in Philadelphia. It's only the people who make them unsafe."

> *-Frank Rizzo, then the mayor of the City of Brotherly Love*

"Smoking kills. If you're killed, you've lost a very important part of your life."

> *- Brooke Shields*

"A verbal contract is not worth the paper it's written on."

> *-Samuel Goldwyn*

"I have opinions of my own --strong opinions-- but I don't always agree with them."
        -George Bush

"A zebra does not change its spots."
        - Al Gore, attacking President George Bush in 1992

"I get to go to lots of overseas places, like Canada."
        - Britney Spears, Pop Singer

"All you have to do is go down to the bottom of your swimming pool and hold your breath."
        - David Miller, US DOE spokesperson, on protecting yourself from nuclear radiation

"Permitted vehicles not allowed."
        - Road sign on US 27

"There is certainly more in the future now than back in 1964."
        - Roger Daltrey, Singer/Actor

"Facts are stupid things."
        - Ronald Reagan

"He's passe. Nobody cares about Mickey anymore. There are whole batches of Mickeys we just can't give away. I think we should phase him out."
        -Roy Disney, Walt Disney's brother, 1937

"Solutions are not the answer."
        - Richard Nixon, former U.S. President

"Elephants Please Stay In Your Car."
　　- Safari park sign

"You can't just let nature run wild."
　　- Wally Hickel, former Secretary Of The Interior

"It was not my class of people. There was not a producer, a press agent, a director, an actor."
　　- Zsa Zsa Gabor, on the jury used
　　for her assault trial

"Reports are sketchy, but we have heard that in the first heart transplant operation in Belgium, both patient and donor are doing fine."
　　- Radio news announcer

"For most people, death comes at the end of their lives."
　　- GLR broadcaster, UK

"Traffic is very heavy at the moment, so if you are thinking of leaving now, you'd better set off a few minutes earlier."
　　- Anonymous Traffic Report

JUST SO YOU KNOW

If you happen to be planning on a career in Korean baseball be advised that the Korea Baseball Organization has officially prohibited wearing frozen cabbage leaves under you cap as a means of keeping cool. Don't say you haven't been warned!

NEVER LET THEM SEE YOUR HAND

In tune with California's laid back attitudes, a holdup man walked into a Modesto bank office without a gun. Instead, he used his thumb and forefinger to show that he meant business. Unfortunately, he neglected to keep his hand in his pocket.

KEY MISTAKE

A Taiwan stock trader accidentally bought $251 million in unintended shares when she mistyped a small order into a computer. The loss on paper amounted to about $12 million, making it one of the most expensive typos ever. The trader is now looking for a new position and in the meantime should bone up on her typing skills.

ZERO TOLERANCE ZERO INTELLIGENCE

A zero tolerance policy to keep weapons out of school in Madison, Wisconsin, lead to a suspension and threat of expulsion for a 6th grader who was a straight "A" student and member of the safety patrol. The boy's offense? He brought a kitchen knife to school so he could slice an onion for a science project. The school officials steadfastly stood by their decision to severely discipline the boy for having a weapon. The 12 year-old said he never considered it a weapon- just a kitchen utensil. Next, they'll be going after the deadly compasses wielded by those crazed geometry students- they may draw a nice circle but those points can be murder.

SPORTS SHORTS- TAKE TWO

Pop star Christina Aguilera was once introduced to golf superstar Tiger Woods. "Oh, Christina," said Tiger, "I love your music. I have all your CDs."

"Sorry, I don't follow tennis," Aguilera replied, "so I don't know much about you."

"I watch a lot of baseball on the radio."
            -Former president Gerald Ford

"We lost a big void."
            - Then Red Sox pitcher Roger Clemens, in 1992,
            on the death of team owner Jean Yawkey

"Always go to other people's funerals, otherwise they won't come to yours."
            -Yogi Berra

"You mean now?"
            -Yogi Berra, when asked what time it was

"I have two weapons – my legs, my arm and my brains."
            -Michael Vick, Atlanta Falcons quarterback

Slugger Dave Kingman once wrapped up a gift for a female sportswriter with whom he had several disagreements. She thought the gift was probably a plea for forgiveness. Think again. She opened up the gift to find a dirty, rotten rat.

Golfer Roberto DeVicenzo's unfortunate legacy will be as the man who signed an incorrect scorecard at the 1968 Masters Tournament. As a result, he lost the championship to the would've been runner-up, Bob Goalby.

On November 19, 1978, with just 28 seconds left on the clock and the ball in their possession, all the New York Giants had to do was fall on the ball for a 17-12 win over the Philadelphia Eagles. But nooo, offensive coach Bob Gibson decided to call for a running play. Quarterback Joe Pisarcik and fullback Larry Csonka got tangled up, the ball was fumbled, Eagles defensive back Herm Edwards scooped it up and ran it in for a touchdown. By the way, Gibson was fired.

On November 17, 1968, the New York Jets were leading the Oakland Raiders 32-29 with less than 65 seconds left in the game, when NBC decided to cut to a new movie version of *Heidi*. Meanwhile, the Raiders went on to score twice to defeat the Jets in what would later infamously become known as the "Heidi Game."

Middleweight champ Sugar Ray Leonard registered a technical knockout over Tom Kelly on October 6, 1978. But Kelly wasn't his opponent- he was the referee. Leonard was fighting Randy Shields when Kelly stepped in the way of a Leonard hook in Round 9 which knocked him silly and split open his eye. Kelly had to be replaced for the tenth and final round by a substitute. On a lesser note, Leonard won the decision.

At the beginning of overtime during a Lions-Steelers Thanksgiving Day game, Steelers captain Jerome Bettis called the flip, which sounded like "tails." Referee Phil Luckett, however, thought he heard Bettis call "heads" and awarded the toss to the Lions. The Lions chose to receive, drove downfield and kicked a winning field goal.

On May 25, 1965, Muhammad Ali knocked out Sonny Liston in the first round of their championship rematch. People wonder, however, who was more embarrassed that night in Maine, Liston or Robert Goulet. The Canadian-born singer forgot the words to the *Star Spangled Banner* while singing before the fight.

Adams Golf Ltd. claimed Nick Faldo to be in breach of his contract. The company said that Faldo had refused to play the Faldo Series wedge – designed by none other than Faldo himself.

In a 1999 NFL game between the Jaguars and the Browns, referee Jeff Triplette called a penalty on Cleveland's Orlando Brown. Triplette accidentally threw the flag directly into Brown's right eye. After leaving the field injured, Brown later came back to the field and shoved Triplette to the ground.

In the 1954 Cotton Bowl, Rice running back Dicky Moegle took a pitchout on his own five yard line and raced along the sideline with nothing but paydirt in front of him. Suddenly, however, Alabama's Tommy Lewis came off the bench and tackled him. The officials awarded Moegle the touchdown and Rice won the game, 28-6.

"He signed with us just to get an engineering education, and that's the wrong reason. I wish he would have told us sooner."

-Coach Danny Ford, on why one of his University of Arkansas freshmen was giving up his athletic scholarship and going home

Just about everyone knows of the "Battle of Buckner Hill" but no blooper book would be complete without it. With two outs in the bottom of the 10th inning of the 1986 World Series between the Red Sox and the Mets, a ground ball went through the legs of Boston first baseman Bill Buckner. The error cost the Red Sox the game and eventually the Series.

In 2002, Mets leftfielder Benny Agbayana caught a fly ball for the second out of the inning. Trouble was, he thought it was the third out and threw the ball into the stands, allowing the San Francisco Giants to score two runs on the mental lapse.

The *St. Louis Post-Dispatch* once featured this golf headline: "Shot off Woman's Leg Helps Nicklaus to 66."

Rosie Ruiz was the winner of the 1980 women's Boston Marathon – temporarily. A neophyte runner, she came out of nowhere to win it. Race experts became suspicious after Ruiz, a complete unknown, had just run the third fastest marathon in women's history. A check of videotapes showed no sign of Ruiz at various race checkpoints. Officials determined that Ruiz had started the race normally but then hopped a subway to a spot near the marathon's finish line where she then slipped back onto the street and ran to glory. She was disqualified and the victory was given to Jacqueline Gareau of Canada.

In order to finance the play *No No Nanette*, Boston Red Sox owner Harry Frazee dealt Babe Ruth to the New York Yankees in 1920. This became known as the "Curse of the Bambino" to the everlasting dismay of Boston fans, that is, until they won the 2004 World Series.

Long before he got into big trouble for tax evasion, Pete Rose got into a little trouble for parking illegally outside Cincinnati's Riverfront Stadium. The street name on the ticket … Pete Rose Way.

While at Notre Dame in 1970, quarterback Joe Theismann changed the pronunciation of his name from "Theez-man" to "Thighs-man" so it would rhyme with Heisman – as in the trophy. Unfortunately for "Thighs-man," the 1970 Heisman winner pronounced his name "Plunkett."

Former President Clinton admitted that, while he was governor of Arkansas, he claimed he didn't feel well one day so he cancelled a couple of appointments and, instead, went out and played a round of golf. During it, he holed a three-iron from behind a tree for an eagle but couldn't tell anyone because he'd said he was ill.

A Polish citizen living in America, Stella Walsh took the gold medal in the women's 100-meter dash at the 1932 Olympics. In 1980, Walsh was shot and killed in Cleveland, an innocent bystander to a fouled up shopping center robbery. An autopsy revealed an astonishing fact- she was a he.